# TUK-TUK FOR TWO

## TWO STRANGERS, ONE UNFORGETTABLE RACE THROUGH INDIA IN A TUK-TUK NAMED WINNIE

ADAM FLETCHER

Copyright © 2020 by Adam Fletcher

All rights reserved.

No part of this book may be reproduced in any form or by any electronic or mechanical means, including information storage and retrieval systems, without written permission from the author, except for the use of brief quotations in a book review.

**Author's Note:**

This book is based on a true story. Everyone in it is real, and so I've changed all names and several other identifying details, I hope for obvious reasons.

024 Retired Not Expired
RICKSHAW CHALLENGE
023 Win Diesel - The Last & The Curious
RICKSHAW CHALLENGE
TN02
Y 6293

# 1

## TRIVANDRUM, INDIA

People used to go places slowly, ponderously, respectfully, on weary feet, in heavy boats, atop trusty steeds, or hugging the lumps of their camels. Inching forwards through the ridges of ancient maps, they'd slowly acclimate themselves to their destination.

Not anymore...

Now, we're slingshot around the globe in winged toothpaste tubes and land dazed and confused, blinking up into suns and seasons to which we do not belong.

Yesterday, it was winter. Today, the world scorched, shimmered, and stalked. It was trying to end me—or, at the very least, make me retreat inside to wave the white flag of air conditioning.

*Where was I?*

*Why was I?*

Wasn't I supposed to stay put in Berlin? To roll out a soft carpet of routine between my office and home and walk back and forth upon it? How had I ended up in yet another city I didn't know how to spell? Standing confused and uncertain in the muddy playground of an all-girls high school?

Circumstance owed me an apology.

Or an explanation, at the very least.

I pulled down on the front of my baseball cap and looked over at Evelyn.

It was her fault.

It was all her fault.

This she-devil standing there innocently fanning the bottom of her fitted white T-shirt, circulating air up her torso. I stole a glance at her stomach and felt as if my insides were being stirred with a stick.

"Welcome, you stupid, stupid people," said the short, squat man at the centre of a huddle of fifty wannabee tuk-tuk-racers. A wide, toothy smile ripped across his face.

Most smiles are warm and inviting. Most smiles trigger chain reactions of happiness. This was not one of those smiles. This was the bottomless-abyss grin of the sadist. A smile that said *I'm going to enjoy this precisely because I know you won't*.

The man flapped up a hand and nudged his purple sunglasses up his aquiline nose. "I'm Aarav. This is India. There are just three rules to survive what's coming. Rule number one: Forget logic. The British spent two hundred years trying to teach it to us. Think you'll crack it in a week?"

Nervous laughter rippled through the crowd. "Things work differently here. When they work at all." He laughed, entirely from his nose. "In theory, there are two sides of the road, but people here don't respect that. That's what you wanted, right? Chaos?"

Had I wanted chaos? I checked with myself...

*Chaos!* I shouted through the caverns of my interior. Anyone in here order chaos?

*No,* was the emphatic answer.

I was here for three reasons:

1. Her
2. My fear of driving

3. Immersion therapy.

I'd once seen a TV show that said if you have a fear, you can spend a lot of hours lying around on an overqualified person's couch trying to make it all your parents' fault, or you can turn, flash your teeth, and scream into fear's stupid face.

In the show, they locked a woman terrified of dogs in a tiny shed with a growling, slobbering Alsatian. The next thirty minutes were not the best of her life, as attested to by her screams and sobs. The dog didn't seem to enjoy it all that much either.

Afterwards, she reported being much less scared of man's best friend. She might have become more scared of sheds, though.

And TV shows.

And immersion therapy.

But let's focus on the fact that she was much less scared of dogs.

*That* was why I was here: to cure my fear of driving. And, perhaps, women. A beautiful stranger and I were about to get into a tiny, three-wheeled, motorised shed and race it across a growling, slobbering India.

"Just because a junction is coming up," Aarav continued, "don't expect that people will brake for it. You know those white lane markings on the road? They're there because we had some spare paint lying around." He chuckled, enjoying our rapt attention.

"Rule number two: Smile. No matter who you crash into, smile and all will be forgiven."

Evelyn leaned in. "Does it worry you he didn't say *if* you crash?"

It did. A lot.

"Rule number three: Wear your badge at all times. Indians are afraid of people with badges. Now, I intend to spend most of the next week drunk and laughing at you all, so you'll mostly deal with my capable assistant here, Pamir." He gestured towards a man every bit as tall as Aarav was short, lean as Aarav was wide, and calm as Aarav was exuberant. Pamir had a narrow white moustache that reminded me of a shoe brush, and he was so tall and lean that his head swayed on top of his body as he walked. Together, they looked like an ill-suited crime-solving double act.

"Thanks, Aarav. Rule number four: When the sun goes down, Indians become monsters. So, you need to make flag-down before dark or you'll lose all the day's points. Questions?"

"How do you drive one?" someone shouted.

Aarav and Pamir laughed. "Don't worry about that," Pamir said, pulling on the ends of his moustache. "Even kids can drive them. We start when we're five years old." He ambled through the crowd to the row of twenty-four multicoloured tuk-tuks. In India, they're usually called rickshaws or autorickshaws, but I've always known them by their much cuter South East Asian name.

Four gears.

Three seats.

A two-stroke engine.

One loud horn.

Zero seatbelts.

And brakes spongier than sponge cake.

He stopped at the one nearest to us, which was painted in the style of a Union Jack. Tuk-tuks are Wendy houses on wheels. Pamir was as large as regret is long. How was he going to fit? He took hold of the frame, concertinaed himself down, and slid across into the driver's seat. By the time he was inside, he had more folds than an origami swan. He gripped the narrow steering column and twisted the grip on its left side. "This is gears."

He twisted the dial on the right. "This gas. To start, pull the starter lever."

To the left of the driver's seat was a lever about seventy centimetres long. With the flick of a practised wrist he jerked it upwards. The engine rumbled to life. "*Easy*. Foot pedal on the left clutch, right brake."

He was economical with words, as if paying by the letter.

"Give gas, dial to first, off clutch."

The tuk-tuk, hypnotised, glided forwards. He stopped, killed the engine, bounced back across the seat, and unfurled himself before us like a ship dropping its sails. The whole demo had taken less than a minute. *Could it be that easy? Was anything that easy? Other than crippling failure?*

Aarav cracked open a beer. "All right then gang. Your turn."

## 2

# BERLIN, GERMANY, SIX DAYS EARLIER

The dark bar was very good at what it did, which was to look like it was doing absolutely nothing at all. That it was here for itself, not you. Did you want something? Well, it would try its best, but it wasn't going to make any promises. Warm yellow light shimmered from candles that might have predated the Enlightenment itself, given how much wax had accumulated at their bases.

It was named after a communist.

It was very good at making money.

I stretched, letting out a contented sigh. It had been a great day. It had been a great day for several weeks straight. Very, very occasionally you notice that you have all the plates of existence up and spinning effortlessly. You have the sense that life is not happening to you, but you're happening to it. That it's a TV and you hold its remote.

My wanderlust slaked, on account of my having spent most of the last few years travelling, I'd decided to never leave Berlin again. I'd spent the past five months renovating an apartment, reinvigorating dwindling friendships, and reinventing myself.

I was doing me.

I was following my bliss.

I was being the change I wanted to see... *in myself*.

After nearly a decade with my previous partner, Annett, I was now relishing being single. I was the sole custodian of my happiness. In the fortress of the self, I took that happiness, locked it in a heavy trunk, dragged it all the way up the spiral staircase to the highest room of the tallest tower, and locked it in. Then, I swallowed the only key.

It was mine. All mine.

The door to the bar opened, and a woman entered.

I looked.

I looked again.

I looked again again: a double double take.

Some women turn heads. This one creaked necks.

She seemed to have her own light source, and it flooded the dingy bar in fifty shades of loveliness. Her head held an impossibly thick tumble of hair the colour of sunflowers at sunset in San Marino. Her face was a triumph of oval symmetry. Her skin the colour of falling snow. Her body wrapped tight in a yellow-and-white-striped dress, sitting over brown knee-high boots and dark grey tights. She had a figure that would make Betty Boop blush.

She stopped time and then laughed at it.

There was no denying it: I'd fallen in lust at first sight.

The door closed behind her with a soft clunk. Phone clasped to her ear, she walked towards the bar, caught her heel on the mat, tripped slightly, and spun around as if to tell it off. Seeing two people arriving, she jumped back to reopen the heavy door and grazed her hip on the edge of a table. A lazy observer might have written her off as clumsy, but that wasn't it. She was just committed to doing everything, all at once, without help.

My imagination rolled up its sleeves, got out its pens and

paper, and scribbled a romantic-comedy-worthy plot for what would now happen.

She'd walk towards me. "Nathan?" she'd say.

I'd nod. For her, I'd be anyone.

She'd sit. We'd talk. There'd be more fireworks than on New Year's Eve. Our conversation would party like it's 1999. Then her actual date would arrive. He'd be a real man: the shoulders of a gladiator, smile of an alligator, hair of a senator, charm of an A-list actor, and certainty of a despot dictator.

I'd apologise. We'd all laugh. I'd move. He'd sit. They'd talk…

It would be stilted. We'd make occasional eye contact, she and I. She'd go to the bathroom and fake a call. An emergency.

"Sorry, Nathan," she'd say. "I've got to run. Let's do this again soon."

She'd signal me as she left and I'd follow her out. We'd crouch behind a parked car. "This is weird, isn't it?" she'd say.

"No," I'd reply. "Everything but this is weird. This—this feels spectacularly right."

It was a beautiful fantasy. I showered in it for a moment and then reached for imagination's tap and turned it off. Real life is not a romantic comedy. Real life is a Greek tragedy in eighty exquisitely underwhelming parts. And man-shaped boys like me are invisible to starlet-shaped women like her.

I returned to my Kindle, retreating to the safety of lives more interesting than my own.

"I know I've said this many times," a voice said, in German. I looked up. "But we're getting drawn into issues not important to our base." It was the beautiful blonde yeti. She slid into the seat next to mine. Our backs were to a wall of white-painted bricks, and we look towards a high purple counter covered in framed black-and-white family photos.

*How many of those people met in bars?* I wondered.

The waiter arrived as she ended her call.

"I'm waiting for someone," she said. "I'll start with a wine, I guess? A wine. Yes. Whatever's driest."

I tried to focus on my book, but its words swirled in a cloud of digital dyslexia.

Fifteen minutes crawled past on its elbows. I spent the time wriggling on my seat as if stung by a squadron of invisible bees. The seat opposite her stayed empty. She passed the time whizzing around her phone at the speed of an in-love Japanese teenager.

Who stood up a woman like her?

Maybe she'd like some company? We could have one of those new-fangled whatchamacallits? *Conversations*, that was it. People had conversations all the time. Nothing to it—just a matter of throwing words into the gaps between us until they're bridged and we can walk across into each other's minds.

I coughed.

I swallowed.

I checked the door to see if her Nathan was arriving. She placed her phone on the table and reached for her wine, a drink she was consuming as if her throat were a raging bush fire.

She'd leave soon.

I opened my mouth.

I closed my mouth.

"St...ood up?" I said, the words tripping over my teeth, smacking into my lips, and landing face first between us as deflated as two-week-old helium balloons. She turned her head, unsure what I'd said and if it had been directed at her. "Sorry?"

"*Erm.*" I cleared my throat and tried to summon conviction. "Stood up?"

The end of her nose twitched. "I'm sat."

"No, I mean..." I nodded to the empty chair.

She angled her face enough for one eye's worth of contact but not enough to confirm her official attendance in the conversation. "I know what you meant."

"*Ah*. That was a joke?"

She risked a full ninety-degree neck swivel, then winked. "It was." The wink—the mullet of facial expressions—was long overdue a comeback. I was happy for the wink. I gave her my best open-mouthed smile. I wanted her to know that while I had none of my hair, I had all my pearly whites. "Good one," I said. Then my mind went blank. I groped for a word. Any word. "...Well," I announced, as if it carried enough meaning for a whole sentence. No words followed it.

This was going terribly. She turned forwards slowly.

Had there been an actual well around, I'd have jumped into it. But then she turned back a little. Stopped. Twisted forwards again. You could almost hear her running the math, crunching the odds, calculating the risks: *Is he a pest? Will I be able to get rid of him if I engage with him?*

I had a Kindle and all my teeth—how weird could I be?

"You know, you kind of look like that actor," she said. "Oh, what's his name?"

"Stanley Tucci."

"No. He starred in... oh a bunch of movies, really. *Transformers*? Not that I've seen *Transformers*. Why am I talking about *Transformers*? Okay, so I watched the first half on a plane." She talked like she walked, words tripping over each other in a rush to get out into the world; a mix of self-conscious and stream of consciousness.

"Stanley Tucci," I repeated. If I had a euro for every time I'd had this conversation since I went bald, I'd be able to afford enough acting lessons to *become* Stanley Tucci.

"No." She zipped around her phone again. "Well... will you look at that." She held it up to my face. "*Stanley Tucci*."

"He's twenty-two years older than me."

"He is?" Her eyes darted for the corner. The wine had flushed colour into her pale cheeks, like the first day of spring.

"Sorry."

"It's fine. There are worse comparisons."

"I once dated a guy who told me I looked like a young Bette Midler."

I turned to better scrutinise her face. "I can see that," I said, pretending I knew who Bette Midler was, young or old.

We were now turned towards each other. I saw that while her face had all the same basic components as other faces, it had been upgraded at check-in and now sat sipping champagne, eating caviar, and swinging its flawless legs amid the ample leg room on offer in genetic first class. Her small, icy blue eyes contained an entire tundra. She was a magic trick that sawed me in half.

Now, I don't want to give the impression she was perfect. That would insult your intelligence and reduce her to mere caricature. No, her incisors curled just slightly forward, her cheeks were lightly pimpled, and thick lines had been cut under her eyes by the scalpel of lost sleep. But who wants perfection? It's untrustworthy. Life scars us, and those scars should show.

On her, they were barely a scratch.

The door opened, and she turned towards it. I took this as my cue to slip out to the bathroom, where I stood at the urinal whistling Europe's seminal 1980s classic "The Final Countdown." If there is a more satisfying song to whistle, I've yet to find it. I enjoyed the sweet taste of having done something scary that had gone okay enough. She and I had enjoyed a short, slightly awkward conversation. But there are worse things than awkwardness. Her Nathan would now arrive and our ships would pass back into the separate channels of our lives.

Mine would stay in control. Those plates would continue

to spin without effort. The contents of that chest, locked up high in that fortress, would remain closed and mine.

There would be many more lusts at first sights.

I walked back towards our tables and found Young Bette Midler still very much alone. As I reached the seat opposite her, some part of me grabbed all the other parts of me and shoved them down into that seat so fast that the world spun.

What part had grabbed me? I'm not sure. The devil on my shoulder, perhaps. My guardian angel, maybe. My runaway ego, possibly. Or my libido, the madman to which I've been chained since I was fourteen.

It was probably my libido.

"Oh," she said, her eyes narrowing. "So. *Okay.*"

3

## TUK-TUK TRAINING, PART ONE

It was like a scene from *The Italian Job*: twenty-four tiny, freshly painted tuk-tuks in a row, as if just removed from their boxes, begging for a spin through the dirt.

Someone had already blown all their bloody doors off.

Opposite them, side by side, stood Evelyn and I—individuals long out of our respective packaging. Two strangers showing all the scuff marks, wear and tear, and emotional scarring of thirty years spent mishandling ourselves. Today, jet-lagged, we wanted only sleep. The other teams had already scampered off to meet their tuk-tuks. I tried to lift my feet but found my flip-flops filled with concrete. Evelyn's head hung forwards in resignation. I understood *my* trepidation, but shouldn't she have been more enthusiastic about the race? She'd been floating on this *Titanic* of an idea long before the rumours of icebergs. I'd hopped the railing at the last minute —after the band had stopped playing, the buffet had been ransacked, women and children had been settled in lifeboats, and Jack and Rose had left steamy handprints in other people's cars.

"So," she said. "Shall we?"

Each tuk-tuk featured a team name on its front and side.

*Team Four: The Inglorious Bembel Boys*
*Team Six: Wat Wen Wong?*
*Team Twelve: The Tuk-Tuk Trolls*
*Team Eighteen: Crouching Woman, Hidden Cucumber*

We walked along the line to the far end, to a tuk-tuk painted azure blue.

*Team 23: Win Diesel – the Last and the Curious*

"Your creation or Juliane's?" Juliane was Evelyn's real racing partner. The person who should have been here. The person I was standing in for.

"Mine."

"A fine effort."

She curtsied. Who would be the first to drive? Her, I assumed, because this was all her idea. Or Juliane's. Either way: not mine. She broke eye contact and stepped past me towards the backseat.

*Okay then.*

During the five-day race, three mechanics would support us. One sauntered over and sat on a low wall behind our tuk-tuk. He stared up at the sky and let out a wide yawn before resting his head against the trunk of a tree. He seemed certain he wouldn't be needed.

Evelyn was already squashed into the backseat.

Which left me with the front.

Which left me with the driving.

My throat swung shut. The only thing squeezing through it were gulps of hot fear—fear I couldn't let her see.

I shuffled forwards, turned to the side, bent as if to touch my knees, and squeezed across into a driver's seat hot enough to fry a steak. I wiped sweat from my eyes and grabbed the steering column. I turned it and felt the front wheel track it, digging grooves into the ground. I tested the switches, fondling everything with the certainty of a virgin lover in a cinema's back row. My hands trembled on the gearshift and accelerator as I looked through the windshield at the dome-shaped playground.

"Both dials turn, so that's good," I said, in my best calm-person voice. I'd spent my life projecting confidence and was good at it. Stanley Tucci good.

"Now I just pull this lever thing, right?" I yanked the starter lever upwards. Unimpressed with my technique, it sank back to the floor. The engine remained eerily silent.

Evelyn leaned over to the front. Tuk-tuks are so small, she could almost have driven it from the back. "Give it a bit of *oomph*."

"All right, backseat driver."

I yanked the lever again. This time, the tuk-tuk jolted forwards as the engine continued its strict vow of silence.

I tried the lever again.

Nothing.

Then again.

Nothing.

I shook out my arm, which was aching, adding itself to an already formidable collection of my discontents. "Is it in neutral?" she asked, leaning further over my right shoulder to turn the dial for herself. Her chest pushing into my shoulder was a distraction I didn't need.

I slid forwards. "It's hard to tell. I think there were markings on the grip, but they've worn off."

A few tuk-tuks were now hopping and wheezing around the field like asthmatic kangaroos. The whole scene looked like the punchline of a joke beginning *How many white people does it take to...*

We needed help. I hung my head out the left side of the tuk-tuk and grinned at the mechanic, my eyes silently screaming.

His refused to listen.

I upped the ante with a wave. Who can resist a wave?

He resisted my wave.

I waved again. I waved harder.

He didn't waver.

I waved more.

He clicked his jaw and stretched his arms across his chest.

I began doing everything all at once: waving, pointing, shouting, gesticulating, floundering.

He rolled a corner of his mouth up towards his ear. *Must he?*

I pointed at him, then at us: *He must.*

He stood, kicked a stone, clicked his back, and perambulated towards us with the gait of a man without a care in the world, a man inhabiting a world in which caring was as obsolete as floppy disks full of pager numbers.

He stopped to the left of the tuk-tuk. He had fantastic, dense hair that clumped at his right temple. Before I went bald, I never paid attention to hair. It was just clutter; an organic hat. Now it got all my attention. It was a big part of why I was so attracted to Evelyn—she had the hair of seven women combined and then lightly electrocuted.

Below this man's hair sat a wide face; a broad canvas on which he could paint.

It was blank. "Yes?"

"It won't start," I said. "I've tried everything. Nothing works." I nodded at the controls. "What am I doing wrong? *Argh.*"

The mechanic blinked.

The mechanic blinked.

The mechanic blinked.

He pushed out his lips.

He leaned down.

He gripped the starter lever.

"Neutrallevergassee?" The word zipped from his lips and past my ears before my mind had time to intercept it.

"Err. Sorry?"

"Neutrallevergassee?"

Did he move so slowly to compensate for how fast he talked? He glided the starter lever upwards and the tuk-tuk's fickle engine—charmed by this man's slow embrace—spurted to life. He leaned across my chest and twisted the accelerator grip. The tuk-tuk purred like a cat before an open fire.

"Neutrallevergassee? Keepgassee?"

He let go of the dial and the engine coughed then lost its voice.

"Can you perhaps do that again, but much, much slower?"

He repeated this magic trick of movements and the engine awoke from its coma. "Neutral.Lever.Gas.See? Keepgassee?"

I looked back at Evelyn. Even covered in a thick layer of sweat, grime, and panic she was a disgustingly beautiful human. It seemed as if, at all times, her chromosomes were bragging. "I don't think he can explain it," she said, in German. "I don't think he's thinking when he's doing it."

The mechanic yawned. We were keeping him up. I took his right hand and placed it over my left, which was wrapped around the starter lever. It was almost exactly the pottery scene in *Ghost*, only with a little more erotic tension.

Together, we gripped. Together, we yanked. Nothing happened.

"No." He pushed my hand away and then regripped the lever and thrust it upwards, just as we had done but garnering the exact opposite result. Aroused, the engine murmured. It wanted more. It had always loved the pottery scene best.

"Neutral. Lever. Gas. See?"

I saw, but I did not see. I retook the lever and propelled it upwards. Nothing.

He did it... worked.
I did it... nothing.
He did it... worked.
I did it... *WORKED!*

"Woah!" I said, as Evelyn whooped and the engine growled, wheezed, then puttered out. I put my head in my hands.

By now, almost all the other tuk-tuks were in motion: crunchy, juddering, overrevved motion.

I wanted to burst into tears, or perhaps flames, but I also wanted to be strong and masculine and competent in front of Evelyn—a woman I intended to woo by pretending to be someone I was not. I've never understood people's preoccupation with being their authentic selves. My authentic self is the sort of person people cross roads to avoid.

"I guess I could have a go?" she said.

It was about time.

We swapped seats. The mechanic scratched at his earlobe as Evelyn gently nudged the starter lever skyward. It was like watching someone tickle a padlock and expect it to open. The mechanic took it from her, pulled on it, and quickly made the engine moan in delight.

"So now I'm in neutral, right?" she asked, remembering to give it a little gas. "But how do I know that it's in neutral?"

"First." He rotated the gearshift forwards then back. "Neutralsee?"

"Okaaaay. But how do you *know* that?"

He looked at her as if she'd asked how he knew Tuesday followed Monday.

"Firstneutrallevergo, see?"

"Mmm." She paused, searching for more delicate wording. "What are you doing that allows you to know when it's in first, and not neutral?"

The man chewed his lip. We were fish that couldn't swim,

birds without flight, and candy that didn't floss. He sucked in his cheeks. He looked over his shoulder. He stood up and clicked his back once more. Then he sloped away.

Evelyn thudded against the seat back. "I hate this. And we just started this. And there's so much more *this* left."

"Isn't it supposed to be *me* who hates this?"

"Well, I also sort of hate driving. I don't know if I'm afraid of it, like you. Maybe I am. In India, at least. But then who wouldn't be? How are we going to drive here, Adam?"

Her using my name reminded me of how little we still knew each other. I would change that. "We're failing," she said. "I hate failing. I just don't understand how it can be this difficult."

I sighed. "It's us, isn't it?"

"If you ever suspect it's you, it's you."

The field had become a mass of swirling, stuttering vehicles. I felt sorry for every engine involved.

"We need a miracle," I said, as a tuk-tuk skidded to a stop alongside us.

4

# BACK TO BERLIN, AND THE BAR

I sat up straight and thrust out my hand. "Adam."

She glanced down at it then back up at me, deciding what was happening and if she was okay with it. I considered again whether I was a pest.

*No, pests don't wonder if they're pests.*

Slowly, she reached out and took my hand. "Evelyn."

I'd always planned to fall in love with an Eve. "Does anyone ever call you Eve?"

"No."

"How do you feel about the name?"

"Mrs Hitler kind of tarnished it, no?" Eva was the German Eve. "And then the whole apple-snake-double-cross thing. It's probably why I don't like apples, come to think of it."

Evelyn was close enough; I decided. "Wait, who doesn't like apples?"

"What are you, the fruit police?"

"How about gardens? Got a problem with those too?"

"I'm good with gardens. Not good in gardens. I'm all thumbs. And not the green sort. My flatmate and I did a plant project last summer. We'd killed them all by autumn. It was a massacre. *Of neglect.*"

So, she didn't live with a boyfriend.

"Did you get stood up as well?" she asked.

I considered lying to look more popular. "No."

"You often come to bars alone, then?"

"Sure. You don't?"

She let the idea settle. "I mean... well... it can just cause problems sometimes. You can get attention. Then you have to get rid of it. Which can be awkward." Something about the subject was making her uncomfortable. Was it because I had done just this? Was I someone she was wondering how to get rid of? "You hungry? I heard the lasagne here's great."

"I'm vegetarian," I said, which was news to me, her, and all the animals I'd put in my mouth recently. "*Vegan*, even. Mostly."

*Vegan?!* I'd punch a puppy in the face for ice cream. There's a condition called alien hand syndrome where a person's hand develops a will of its own. I seemed to have developed alien tongue syndrome. I was becoming jealous of the person I was pretending to be.

Silence parallel parked between us. We needed a topic quickly, or we'd lose conversational thrust. I needed something that would show her I was an original thinker—fascinating and different, but good different: *turmeric* different not *kombucha* different.

I knew stuff. I had topics. I roamed the shelves of my mind frantically pulling down reels of tape. Everything was blank. Wiped by uncertainty. Stalling for time, I moved my Kindle and notepad across from the other table.

*I'd been reading. What had I been reading?*

"Attractivity!" I blurted. "I'm reading about attractivity."
*Phew.*

She squinted. "Why?"

"I want to be more attractive."

"Why?"

"Erm, it seems better than being less attractive?"

Not something she knew anything about. I tried to think of an anecdote from the book. *The thrust... The losing... We were.*

I pushed my hands out in a cupping motion. "Boobs."

Her eyes dropped to my hands. I followed them down as awkwardness blossomed between us. I pinned my hands to the tabletop. They'd been naughty and needed to be punished.

"*Boobs*," she repeated.

"Boobs," I said. "So, and I never knew this, but men are primarily attracted to signs of fertility. Or so the book says. Small boobs don't sag, right? So they're not a good marker of procreation potential. Men aren't attracted to big boobs—they're attracted to *pert* big boobs. Okay, this is a weird topic."

She jutted out her chin. "I like weird topics. I read a similar thing about blonde hair. It's the only hair colour that darkens as you get older. Bright blonde is basically just shouting I CAN STILL MAKE BABIES!" She tousled her hair. "Or 'I know how to use hair dye,' as in my case."

That was weirdly honest.

She checked the door. She checked her phone again. We were communicating, but our conversation was in a straight-jacket. Help arrived, as it has through time immemorial, in the form of alcohol. The two glasses of white wine we'd ordered separately arrived together, released the conversation's straps, took it by the hand, and guided it along the well-worn small-talk pathways of *where are you from, what do you like about Berlin*, and *what did you want to be before you grew up*.

It was fine, pleasant, but we were obviously not small-talk people.

"I just got back from Rwanda," she said. "Few blondes there."

"How was it?"

"Great, if you're into genocides."

And with that we jumped off the pathway, ran through a bush, tumbled down a hill, and came to a stop before the high fences guarding humanity's Theme Park of the Absurd. With most people I don't jump that fence. They find my interest in cults, dictators, religions, the paranormal, and other things that go bump in the night to be too distasteful.

She wouldn't, I sensed. There was a glint at the edges of those extraordinary eyes; shining tracers of mischief.

"Don't tell anyone," I said. "But I'm a bit of a dark tourist."

"Ha! Me too!"

And over we leapt. We roamed the exhibits for a long time, swapping anecdotes and stories. I didn't want to leave. "Did you know Imelda Marcos had over a thousand pairs of shoes?"

"The Philippine dictator's wife?"

"Yeah," she said. "There's a museum dedicated to her shoes. I've been to it."

"Amazing."

"And she built a palace out of coconuts. She was a little bit. *Nuts*, I mean. It's hard to explain to your family why you're skipping the family holiday in France to go to Nigeria, right?" She paused. "Another weird topic."

"Nigeria? A good topic. Better than the weather and work."

"What do you do for work, and in what weather?"

My laughter was drowned out by a loud cackle of her own. I've a soft spot for people who laugh at their own jokes. If you spend all day with yourself, you might as well enjoy the show.

"I write about weird places," I said.

"I try to make things less weird in places."

"In what way?"

"Politics." She checked her phone again. I swallowed a

lump of irritation.

"I'm a travel writer who's lost interest in travelling, which is like being a politician who's lost interest in…" I paused. "So it turns out I have very little idea what politicians do all day. Kiss babies?"

She signalled the waiter then looked at me. "Another?"

So it couldn't have been going that badly.

"I'm going to India on Wednesday," she said. "I'm racing a tuk-tuk one thousand kilometres in five days."

"Wow. Those things are lethal."

"Like cheating at cards with Saddam Hussein. Juliane, the person I'm supposed to be meeting here, roped me into it. Seems she's gone AWOL."

She checked her phone for the fifteenth time. Her voice had a softer edge now. Alcohol had undone its top button. She looked over at the clock. "Two hours already? Wow. Where the hell is Juliane? I'll just try her again, okay?"

This time Juliane answered. Evelyn stood up and walked towards the door, leaving me to review the detective work I'd done in the case of Her: she hadn't mentioned a boyfriend, she appreciated weird countries, she did stupid challenges, she was a triumph of symmetry, and she was easy to rope into things.

I closed the case. It was official. She was perfect.

There was just one problem: I wasn't perfect. I was, mostly, a missed opportunity in spectacles. Someone pretending to be a man while feeling like a confused toddler alone in the sandpit wondering why no one wants to play with him. I had everything under control? I couldn't even control who walked into my life and made me an instant vegetarian.

She returned and slumped into her seat. "So, I guess I'm not going to India. Juliane's broken her arm, the poor thing. That's why she's not here."

"No way."

"Yep way. Knocked herself out and everything. She's at the

hospital. Kind of ironic that just before we do something dangerous, she crashes her bike into a taxi here in Berlin."

"That sucks. Do you have another friend who could take her spot?"

"At this short notice?"

Wednesday was four days away. "Yeah, it would be a big ask."

"And in my line of work, we don't have time for friends. Just colleagues you drink with."

More radical honesty. She was an open book; I just wasn't sure of its genre. She stroked the bottom of her wine glass. "I really, really need a holiday. I've been working so much. And the race. I don't know if I was looking forward to it—mostly I just found the idea terrifying—but the good stuff is always terrifying, right?"

"Right. Or it's dentistry. Go alone instead?"

"*Pff*. It's so much driving. And India alone? As a blonde woman? *No*."

It's difficult, it takes great concentration, you have to be really, really quiet, but I think, in moments of inner strife, you can hear the different parts of yourself arguing.

A thought arrived at the door of my consciousness.

It knocked.

I ignored it.

It knocked louder.

I ignored it again.

It kicked the door down. *Think me then say me.*

But I don't even know her.

*Yeah, but you want to know her.*

But it's crazy. We just met.

*Aren't you the sort of person who tries to convince people you're the sort of person who does crazy things?*

But I have stuff going on.

*You don't have a single appointment between now and*

*Christmas. And there's a book in this. And you need books.*

I've retired.

*From paying rent?*

Good point.

*Thanks.*

Don't get cocky.

*Sorry. And there's a Her in this.*

Yeah, but that's...

*And you could cure your fear of driving.*

It's a fear for a reason. They're difficult to cure. And it's...

*Terrifying? All the good stuff is terrifying.*

Or dentistry.

*I'm pretty sure this is not dentistry.*

I cleared my throat, but no words emerged from it. She took the last swig of her wine. "Maybe I'll find someone, somehow."

I nodded. Her phone trilled and she jumped in response, trying to remember which pocket she'd put it in. Not that it stayed in her pockets for long.

"Sorry, I've. Oh no."

She said *sorry* a lot.

"Is it always like this?"

"No. Usually it's worse."

"How do you put up with it?"

She held my gaze and her mouth opened then closed as she translated feelings into words. "I got a lot of privileges," she said. "The full set, really. I'm not in any way delusional. I don't think I'm saving the world or anything. But politics is how you fix the most things for the most people. I enjoy going to bed knowing I tried to nudge things a tiny bit in what I hope is the right direction. Know what I mean?"

I thought about my job, which comprised sitting alone in a room writing stories about myself, perhaps the most narcissistic profession imaginable. "I do."

"I'm sure your books mean something to people too."

"Eh. I guess."

She looked down at the flood of messages gushing down her phone's display. "Why would they…" It rang. She got up, mouthing another *sorry* in my direction.

"No," she said, her voice fading out as we walked away. "I'm on a sort of…"

*Did she say date? Have I become her Nathan?*

A few minutes later she returned. She stood beside me, covering the phone's speaker with her hand. "I'm sorry, but some politician has said something stupid about taxing cats."

"Everyone loves tax cuts."

"No. Taxing c-a-t-s! People are crazy about their cats. We'll get crucified. And I should probably go check on Juliane." She looked at our two empty glasses. "This was, err, nice. I've paid the bill."

"You didn't need to." I reached for my wallet. "I'll give—"

"Don't worry about it."

Was it because I'd said I was a writer? Every second person in Berlin is a writer who, despite all their best intentions, never quite gets around to sentence*ing*.

"You sure?"

"Sure."

I ripped a page from my notepad and wrote my number on it. "I might, you know, I mean, who knows, right? Time. I have time. In case you don't find…" I said, hoping she knew what I was saying, no matter how badly I was saying it.

Going to India on such short notice was a pipe dream. Or a pipe nightmare. Some sort of pipe, anyway. Regardless, I wanted to see her again. Her phone disappeared beneath that exquisite mane of golden hair. "Mark. What? No!" She mouthed one last sorry and strode from the now empty bar.

I sank back in my seat. Who had just blown through my life in a whirlwind of loveliness?

5

## TUK-TUK TRAINING, PART TWO

A man bounded out of the tuk-tuk he'd just parked beside us, as I massaged my temples. "You trying to summon a genie?" he said. "Because congrats, pal, it worked!"

The man looked Indian, but his accent was unabashedly British. He was balding, a little overweight, and had a greying scratchy beard that hung from uncooked-pizza-dough cheeks. He turned to Evelyn in the driver's seat and dropped to his haunches. "The most important thing, luv, is that it's in neutral. If it's in first, you're toast. You'd have more luck starting the dead."

*Starting the dead? With Toast?*

I slid out the backseat and stretched just as his female racing partner vaulted into the front seat of their tuk-tuk, gave me a thumbs up, yanked crudely on the starter lever, roughly twisted the gearshift into second-then-first-then-second-then-first, pulled far too quickly off the clutch, and lurched forward. Her engine yelled in protest, and an angry black cloud of exhaust was spat up into my face.

She was moving, at least.

"Neutral sits between first and second," said our saviour.

"Why would it be there, though?" Evelyn asked.

"Beats me sideways. And it's not even a real gear—it's just a tiny notchy thing." He stuck out his tongue. He had a certain jovial, uncle-like quality. His name was Manish, and he'd been born to Indian parents in Leicester.

I got out of the tuk-tuk and was only three steps from it when a tuk-tuk full of rambunctious Australians swerved straight for me. I had to dive back into the vehicle to avoid it. They howled with laughter. I made a mental note to hate them forever.

Manish moved round to the other side of the tuk-tuk. "If the vehicle rolls slightly forwards but doesn't start when you yank this a-here-lever"—he swept his palm over it as if it were the star prize in a TV game show—"you're in first. Which is the *last place* you want to be." He chuckled. "Little racing joke there." He was very casual about our impending doom. "My old man's an amateur race driver. I could drive this thing blindfolded."

"It's like everyone's doing just that," I said.

"Ha. *This guy.*" He took hold of the starter lever. "Come here, lad, and give this a good gripping."

I looked around for incoming tuk-tuks. Tentatively, as though afraid of waking a sleeping baby, I tiptoed to the front of the tuk-tuk, joined Manish at the lever, and took it in my right hand.

"Not so tight. You're not trying to yank it off. Firm but fair is the name of the game. *No.* Looser. *No.* Tighter." He sighed then knocked my arm away. "Okay, let me set the scene. You're fifteen. Your parents are out for the next hour. You're in your bedroom. You're not in a rush. Your trousers are down. What are you doing?"

"Err. This is getting kind of—"

"Gross?" said Evelyn.

"Okay. Prudes." He stopped and scratched the back of his

head. "New metaphor. It's a snake, right? You don't want it to get away *or* for it to bite you. So, you grip it at the neck. But it's wriggling. *Oooh... I'm a snake. I'm a-wriggling.*" He wobbled his hands through the air. "You need to knock it out. To yank its neck back. But you don't want to snap that neck now, do you?"

"Ehm... do I?" I said. "Is it poisonous? Angry? I'm lost. This is a very elaborate metaphor."

"I'm a very elaborate man."

"Have you ever charmed a snake?"

"In *Leicester*?"

He was charming me, at least. I wanted to learn and be equally beguiling in return; to have us snaking our way around this muddy field in our tiny novelty vehicle. And so—in homage to the moment in a martial-arts movie when the protagonist realises things are about to get serious, perhaps even montage-serious—I punched my open palm.

"Woah," said Manish. "It's on."

"Damn right. You're not the only elaborate man in these parts." I retook the lever in my no-longer-to-be-messed-with right hand, gripping it 60 percent as hard as before. With a sharp intake of breath, I thrust it upwards, ending with a deft wrist-flick. Like an ogre after a long nap, the engine grunted awake.

"Whoop whoop!" said Evelyn, increasing the tuk-tuk's growl with a little petrol encouragement.

"Jackpot." Manish brushed dust off invisible lapels. His metaphors were bad, but his results were good. We shifted our attention to the next problem: not stalling. "You've got yourselves an overly sensitive engine," he said. "I'll get that looked at for you, shall I?"

"Can you do anything about the two overly sensitive drivers?" Evelyn shouted, as Manish darted into the storm of tuk-tuks raining down on the centre of the field. He was heading for Aarav and Pamir, who were sitting with the mechanics in the shade cast by the school.

What had we done to deserve such kindness beyond displaying such incredible feebleness? Manish returned with a more engaged mechanic, who undid the back hatch (tuk-tuk engines are in the rear) and turned a single screw three full rotations. Suddenly our engine was happy to idle without constant spurts of petroleum reassurance. Manish retook position, on his haunches, next to the starter lever.

"Your turn, me darlin'."

Evelyn slid across the seat, grabbed the lever with her left hand, and tugged. Nothing.

"Is it in first?" she asked.

"Not your problem, me thinks. 'arder, luv. Your snakes a-wriggling."

She tried again. Nothing.

She swapped hands. Silence.

Manish sucked in air through a gap in his front teeth. "Give it more welly."

"Welly?" she asked. She was German, but her English was so good I often forgot it was an adoptive mother to her tongue.

"Slang," I said. "It's a boot."

"What's it mean, though?"

"It means tug harder."

"I'm tugging harder. *Hard*."

"Really give it some," he said. "You're being too polite."

She tried with two hands; the engine's silence was deafening.

Manish's lips clamped together. We swapped a look of resignation—the snake had got away from her. Or would bite her. Or was dead. Exactly what was happening with the snake continued to confuse me. But I knew that, once again, it had got the better of an Eve... *lyn*.

"I guess I can just do the lever each time?" I said.

"You'll get out in traffic and pull it *every time*?"

I threw up my hands.

"No," she said flatly.

"I don't mind."

"I want to do it myself." She pulled it again. Nothing. Again. Harder. Nothing.

"I will, though."

"No!"

What did it matter? We were a team, weren't we? She grabbed the lever with two hands and began furiously pumping it upwards. "AHHHHHHH. Fuck you! Stupid, stupid lever!"

She wiped away a tear. I wasn't sure how to console her. Or why her needing my help was such a problem. Or how to drive a rickshaw. Or why we'd both agreed to. I knew little, really.

She blinked away another tear. We were yet to complete a single lap.

"That was absolutely hilarious," Aarav said, slapping his belly as everyone returned to the shade for a break. "And I thought Indians couldn't drive!"

I looked down at my hands: filthy and weeping blood, pus, and water from a half-dozen new wounds. I was exhausted, miserable, and melting. How were we going to drive one thousand kilometres when we couldn't drive one?

"Okay, so you all have the basic idea now. The next step is what I like to call 'drive like an idiot.' Because while you're terrible now—did I mention how terrible you are?" He took a long swig from his beer. "You truly are. But in a few days, there will be a click in your silly heads and you'll think *I can do this*. When that happens..." He swung a thumb behind him, over the wall, to the road beyond. "You'll drive like them out there. *Don't*. Take the next fifteen minutes to get all your aggression out. Don't come back without having had at least one crash."

Evelyn shuddered.

"Drive like maniacs! Go!"

*Going is the problem*, I thought, as I got back behind the controls. But thanks to Manish's help, I had the technique down and got us trundling along in first gear, then second, then third. We swirled unpredictably through the field like a late-night drunk dancing around lampposts. "Be careful!" Evelyn said with a moan, fundamentally misunderstanding the point of the whole exercise.

*Crash*, *crunch*, *bang*: four tuk-tuks collided in a heap behind us. Up ahead, the howling Australians were gunning straight for us, their tuk-tuk driven by a giant. All I could see through the windshield were two thick arms and a formidable wall of chest. He looked like an American footballer riding a tricycle. Riding a tricycle right at us.

I would not give in. I would not change course. We advanced upon each other like duelling knights. Who was I kidding? I would give in. I would change course. I was a wuss. But I was also a wuss in mid-gear-change, and second gear was stuck. The engine screamed in anguish, and we slowed to a stop as its power drained. At the last second, the Australian realised I wasn't going to move out of his way and swerved so sharply to avoid me that his tuk-tuk tipped over.

There was a mighty thud. A giant tree had fallen in the forest. I was there to hear it. It made a hell of a sound.

Evelyn leapt out and ran towards the Australians looking whiter than a poltergeist in a blizzard. "I didn't know it was that easy to tip over!" she shouted. I fumbled with the starter lever, then paused. Why hadn't I rushed to help them? It was obviously the right thing to do. I got a small jolt of delight—reflected empathy—at how naturally it had occurred to her. And she was on my team; she'd have my back. I knew I should help too, but if I was there helping them, I couldn't be here helping myself, getting the practice time we badly needed. And they had Evelyn now, and that was more than plenty.

Manish's tuk-tuk bounced past as if it were trying to take flight. He saluted from its backseat. I pulled on the lever, switched to first, and sped away. Minutes later I returned to the crash site at a slow enough speed that Evelyn could run alongside and jump into the back, just in time to avoid Manish's girlfriend, who was driving their tuk-tuk as though it were both invisible and invincible.

"They get out okay?" I asked, as I launched us into second gear.

"You didn't come and help?" The *didn't* landed so firmly it sprained its ankle.

"I figured you had it covered," I said, knowing I'd cast myself in an unfavourable light, one making her consider whether I was the sort of man who'd get up at 4am to mop up the sick of our unborn children. Or was I the only one thinking about our unborn children? I hoped they'd get her hair. Or at least some hair.

"My turn to drive," she said.

A few laps later, we were called back in.

"Very good," said Aarav. "I saw a lot of idiots out there. It's time to get out on the road."

The group murmured and shook its collective head.

"You're ready."

"Have you seen us?" I asked. This was not a moment for projecting confidence. It was a moment for protecting strangers. While India is famed for its vehicular incompetences, it was reckless to inflict us—and perhaps more specifically me—on the innocents of Trivandrum.

"You're ready. Well, not you. But we're out of time."

Pamir twiddled the ends of his moustache. He didn't seem to share Aarav's enthusiasm. Mostly, he looked like a man picking his own pockets. Aarav added a new storey to his grin. "LET'S DO THIS! You're going to whizz back to the hotel. On the way, stop at the train station for a platform ticket. *No maps. No GPS*. If you get lost, ask people. It's the Indian way. I'll give you a clue..." He spun on his heels and pointed. "Twenty minutes that way!"

How could it take twenty minutes to cross a city when it had taken three hours to lap a field?

We were about to find out.

6

# BACK TO BERLIN, TWO DAYS AFTER ADAM MET EVELYN

"Hello," I mumbled into my phone, crawling out of the fog of sleep.

*What time is it? Is it even a time? Who still calls people?*

"So, err, remember me?" Her voice quivered. "*Evelyn. From the bar?*"

I rubbed a crust of sleep from my eye. "Mmmmm," I said, playing what I hoped was cool.

"So." She coughed. "The race. India... Were you *serious*?"

*About racing a tuk-tuk, with a stranger, through the country with the worst traffic in the world? No, of course I wasn't serious.*

"There's a 50 percent chance we'll die. And the flight's in two days. But if you really want to, okay..."

It wasn't a reasonable offer. But then she wasn't a reasonable woman. She was certainly unreasonably attractive and intelligent and funny and angelic and wonderful. I tried not to let that sway me, which was like a hammock trying to remain still in a tornado.

"If I *really want to*?" I said. "You're not exactly making me feel special here. I'd be saving your holiday."

"Pff, you're special, honey. You're the only person flexible enough to do this at such short notice."

I liked the sound of the *honey*. I liked everything about her. I knew very little about her.

"And if you didn't have a horrible time talking to me in the bar..."

Fishing didn't suit her; she was the catch. "I've got a lot of stuff on," I lied.

"Pff, no you don't."

"Stop *pffing* me! You know barely anything about me." Did she want to know things about me? I sure hoped so.

"I'm notoriously perceptive. I think. Am I? *Well*. And I googled you. You *are* a travel writer, so you could use the race for a book, no?"

I looked around my bedroom. My new apartment was perfect. Settled. Ordered. Just waiting for me to stay put and enjoy it.

"It's a hundred euros to change the name on the plane ticket," she continued. "I'm sure you've already had all your injections. There's a same-day emergency visa. I'd send you all the forms. You'd just need to go to the embassy. We'd have separate hotel rooms."

My gaze wandered to the chalkboard to-do list on my bedroom door.

*~~Dancing~~*
*~~New look~~*
*~~Apartment~~*
*Driving?*

I hadn't driven in a decade. It was a dislike that, through neglect, had morphed into a fear. But if I could drive a tuk-tuk, I could drive anything. If I could drive in India, I could drive anywhere. And I'd get to spend ten days with her. Would that be enough time to find out who she was and what she wanted and then convince her to abandon that and want me instead?

"How much would all this cost?"

"Well, Juliane isn't exactly in what you'd call a strong negotiating position right now."

"You're encouraging me to take financial advantage of your one-armed best friend?"

"I just get more intriguing, right?" Her voice dropped to the raspy depths of a Hollywood movie voice-over. "*Two strangers. The race of a lifetime. And now, he must come out of retirement for one last job...*"

Coming out of retirement for one last job? When had that ever gone wrong? The book's blurb practically wrote itself. Not that anyone would believe it.

"The blurb writes itself, don't you think?" she said.

"Oh, goddammit."

## 7

# TUK-TUK TRAINING, PART THREE

Evelyn looked at the playground's open gate, then back at me, then back at the gate. I'd tell her she needed to drive us out of here. I'd be honest, for a change.

Her shoulders curled forwards. "Do you think... maybe... you could drive?"

It had cost her something to ask. I could see that.

"Yeeeaaah," I said breezily. "No problem."

But it was a problem; a gigantic problem; an insurmountable problem; a cold-fusion-sized problem. Driving has always held a special place in the hills of my personal hell. It's just too much responsibility to be on the shoulders, under the feet, and in the hands of someone as fickle and daydreamy as me.

But I also wanted to appear strong and competent. And I wanted to overcome my fear. I wouldn't be able to do either from the backseat.

I got in and looked for a spot on my clothes on which I could dry my hands but found everything soaked through with sweat and grime. I played with the dials while trying to psych myself up. Twenty Indians looked on from the gate, taking photos and making videos. The revolution might not be televised, but our demise just might.

"You can do it," Evelyn mumbled. Was she trying to convince herself or me?

Stress pushed, pulled, squeezed, and shoved my insides around in a mosh pit of uncertainty that left me unable to think, only feel.

I felt shitty. And I remembered why I'd engineered my life to have as little of this sensation as possible. I pulled the lever. The engine rumbled, and I got us rolling ominously towards the open gate, third in the convoy of tuk-tuks.

I turned right, and we began our ascent towards the main road. This was the first time I'd driven anything with gears in a decade. A fat man bounced up and down on my chest as I kept my eyes fixed on the two tuk-tuks in front.

*Don't stall. Don't stall. Don't stall.*

Aarav, Pamir, and the mechanics had taken position at the top of the hill. Spread out across the first half of the road, they were clearing a path for us to get across its five lanes of traffic, squeeze through a gap in the central reservation, and merge into five lanes heading left, in the direction of the train station.

A fine needle was about to be threaded.

*Don't stall. Don't stall. Don't stall.*

If either tuk-tuk in front of me stalled, it would mean a hill start with twenty-one tuk-tuks behind me and fifty Indians watching me. Five lanes of rush-hour traffic would be held up by my incompetence.

The first tuk-tuk cleared the hill.

*Don't stall. Don't stall. Don't stall.*

We neared the top. The engine's grunts intensified as it asked for second gear. I couldn't risk a gear change here, at this angle.

*Don't stall. Don't stall. Don't stall.*

The second tuk-tuk stalled.

*Brake, Adam, brake! How does one brake?*

"Brake!" Evelyn shouted, as I found the brake pedal too late and we thudded into the back of the second-tuk-tuk, then stalled.

"Hey!" its driver shouted.

"Sorry!" I yelled back, as the tuk-tuk behind me stalled, as did the one behind it, then the one behind that, in a Mexican wave of incompetence that rippled back into the playground.

Tuk-tuks don't have a handbrake, so I wedged the pedal all the way to the floor. We were on the steepest part of the hill. Aarav waved me into the road. "Come on, go, go, go!"

My heart slammed repeatedly into the wall of my chest. What was the recipe for a hill start? Extra clutch or extra gas?

*Gas*, I decided, and released all our little go-kart offered. The wheels skidded beneath us, grappling the unforgiving surface, and lurched us forward, over the hill, into the road. We shot past the five lanes of penned-in traffic, through the central reservation, where I remembered I brought us to rest in a gap between two tuk-tuk Taxis.

"What are we doing?" I said.

"You're driving a rickshaw!" answered the driver on my right. He leaned across the narrow gap between our vehicles, flashing me a thousand white teeth. "How do you like it?"

"It's... err, hard?"

He laughed dismissively. "No. *Selfie?*"

A scooter weaved through the traffic and plugged the minuscule gap on our left side. "White people in a rickshaw!" said its driver, a boy barely of drinking age. "Where are you going?"

"To Goa."

"Goa!" He cackled. "So far! You will need to be very careful."

He wasn't wearing a helmet.

"Do you think we'll make it?"

The traffic light flicked to yellow. "No," he said, speeding away.

The realisation of how novel we were in these vehicles relaxed me. One of the best things about being abroad is getting to play the ignorance card. In this culture—one that venerates whiteness—it was more widely accepted than Visa.

A few engine stalls, several near misses, and seventeen selfies later, we pulled into a petrol station for gas. Tuk-tuks need petrol and oil in a specific ratio. As the attendant performed this delicate alchemy, locals held a forecourt meet-and-greet, peppering us with questions and requests for photographic proof that we had, albeit briefly, shared time and space.

I paid the bill and found Evelyn shaking the tuk-tuk to mix the petrol and oil.

"How you doing?"

She took her hands off the frame. "How do I look like I'm doing?"

She looked as if she were hanging halfway out of a lion's mouth. "You look great."

"*Liar*. Mind if I drive?"

"You sure?"

"I hate that I can't do it on my own."

"That doesn't matter."

"It does to me. I think if I don't start driving now, I'm never going to. It will become a *thing*. I hate things."

"I have every confidence in you," I lied. No matter what I'd said back on the playground, I knew that getting out in traffic to tug on the starter lever each time she stalled would be suicide. "If I get run over by something or many things all at once, tell my parents I'm sorry I ignored all their advice, always, as a matter of rule."

Not that they knew I was here. Not that they knew who Evelyn was. My mum would adore Evelyn. She had the beauty of a Disney princess but the brains of a senior Disney corporation lawyer. They mustn't meet; I'd never hear the end of it.

"I haven't even told my parents I'm doing this," she said. "They'd kill me. Assuming this doesn't. And I'm still putting the odds at fifty-fifty."

Evelyn stared down at the controls and gripped them both as if she'd never seen them before and would never let them go. She did a lot of things in this confusing, contradictory manner —as though she had perfect theoretical knowledge of the world but no real-world experience. She was a confident mind trapped in an apprehensive body. Yet she was here, doing things like this, with near strangers like me. It was part of why I found her so intriguing. My job forces me to caricature people. To trap the complex and unknowable about a person into a prison cell of twenty-six rearrangeable blocks. Yet she kept breaking free somehow—digging a hole, picking a lock, bribing a guard, jumping a fence. She kept escaping my expectations.

"You can do this," I said.

"I can do this," she whispered.

"You can do this!" I climbed into the back.

"I CAN DO THIS!"

She slid into first gear and swung off the clutch, and we whiplashed our way out of the forecourt.

"Oh God. Oh God. I'm doing this!"

"Watch out!" She swerved left then right through a chicane of scooters.

"I hate this. I hate this. I hate this!" she shouted, as we approached our first roundabout. Germany is too direct a culture to have something as nonconfrontational as roundabouts.

"Which way round do I go?"

"Have you ever driven in left-hand traffic?"

"No."

## 8

# BACK TO TEGEL AIRPORT, ON THE WAY TO INDIA

As ideas went, this one made about as much sense as getting a face tattoo of your own face. Who was she? Why had she agreed to this? Why had I agreed to this? What had I agreed to? I slid into the red-vinyl booth of the airport's American-themed diner. "This feels like an arranged marriage."

"America?"

"Us."

"Oh. Well. More for you than me. I know your whole life story already."

"How?"

"Google."

I'd googled her, too, but there wasn't much to find. Plus, I'd been busy chasing the rabbit of international bureaucracy through the warrens of the Indian embassy—an embassy that operated with as staunch a commitment to disorder as the country itself. At each step, I assumed something would stop me, turn me round, pat me on the behind, and send me back to my ordered, in-control life.

Secretly, I had wanted something to do just that. To give me a way out without my having to lose face; my Stanley

Tucci–impersonator's face. Instead, when problems had presented themselves, I'd simply paid to make them go away, or charmed people with the story of the stupid thing I was about to do with the person I didn't know.

And so now I was sitting—a bulging sports holdall at my feet and an expensive emergency visa in my passport—opposite a woman whose presence was as intoxicating as three back-to-back shots. And then slapping the bar and asking for three more.

"I have this friend," she said. "Anton. Nice suits. Good dresser, Anton."

*Is she saying I'm not a good dresser? Am I a good dresser? Who is this Anton guy? Has she slept with Anton? Is she still sleeping with Anton? Why do I have all these horrible thoughts in my head and how can I get them out?*

We rarely discuss male jealousy in popular culture. It's considered more shameful than its female equivalent. When we see it ripping through a relationship, it's always in a destructive, masculine-approved form—shouting, controlling, emotional strong-arming, or outright violence. I am a jealous man, but this is not the shape of my jealousy. I don't scream or shout. I don't punch, kick, or threaten. I don't try to change, control, or surveil. My jealousy is an act of violence, but it's always directed inward, at myself.

It's... imagine a glass bottle, blue, with an aged cork. On its label is a black skull and crossbones, and under is one word, in all caps: *DOUBT*. In that bottle is poison. Whenever I feel jealous, an icy hand grips that bottle, yanks free its cork, wrenches open my mouth, and pours that poison into me...

Doubt that my partner really loves me.

Doubt that I really love them.

Doubt that they are who they say they are.

Doubt that they feel what they say they feel.

Doubt that I feel what I say I feel.

Doubt that I deserve them.

Doubt that they deserve me.

It's not discerning, the doubt. It has just one desire: it wants them gone. It thinks it's protecting me, helping me, returning order and control to my life. Jealousy is love's antidote—a poison that makes it so sick and twisted that it curls up and dies. It had been a long time since I was at the start of a relationship and not in its cuddly, predictable middle. Suddenly I remembered all the uncertainty, anxiety, excitement, confusion, and doubt of a beginning.

The doubt, mostly.

I closed my eyes. I wasn't ready for this. I felt as if I'd opened a window to let in some fresh air and had been blown halfway across the city by Hurricane Her.

"You okay?" she asked.

I opened them. "Sorry?"

"Lost you there?"

I tried to focus. "No no. Carry on..."

"*Anton*. Lives in Cologne. Fun city. You been to Cologne?"

"Sure."

"So, he meets this girl in a club. They hit it off and swap numbers and I—*she* gets home and her phone beeps. It's him. The message is just three words: *Breakfast in France?*

"She sends him back a thumbs up and a picture of a croissant. Thirty minutes later, they're in his smart Audi. The city fades out and the motorway tumbles open before them. They're revelling in their spontaneity, you know? In the moment. But also, already past it and thinking how they will tell its story in the future."

She lifts a hand and bounces each word: "Breakfast. In. France."

I smiled. I was in that car with them. Story is the cleanest drug, the greatest high, university for the soul.

"During that drive, she says some things. I don't remember what, maybe that she's an anti-vaxxer or shops at Goop or something, but it becomes clear to Anton he's wrong about her. That it would never work between them. That she's not his type."

I frowned. "Awkward. Do you have a type?"

"Yeah, awkward," she said, sidestepping the question. "It gets worse and worse though, and somewhere in Belgium, he decides he just can't take it anymore. Can't make it to France. Just has to be rid of her right there and then. He sees a sign for a train station and follows it. He pulls in. 'I'm sorry,' he says. 'This was a mistake. This will not work.'"

I blew out a lungful of air. "Dumped in Belgium. Harsh. Dumped in France and at least you've good wine, cheese—"

"People to shrug with."

We laughed. "But Belgium?"

"*Belgium.*" She nodded. "So, 'Fine,' she says, 'let's just have a nice breakfast in France and go back then?' But he's blunt, Anton. 'Yeah, about that. I think you should take the train home.' She's furious but what's she going to do? Refuse to leave the car? No. She's got her dignity. Or what's left of it. She gets out. But it's really early. There are no trains. And it's Belgium."

"*Belgium.*"

"So she sits on the platform and waits. No wine, no cheese, probably some shrugging. He drives on to France on his own, eats a croissant in Lille, comes back."

"Why are you telling me this story?" I paused. "*Oh.* We're the... *I'm* the..."

"Welcome to the context."

We were about to go much further than France together. "Evelyn, I have something to tell you."

Her face twisted. "You snore? You're a murderer? Both?"

"Both. But I only snore if I drink a lot."

"Wait." She scowled. "You're a murderer?"

"That's what I wanted to talk to you about."

"Men—only good for one thing and rarely good at that."

"No. I mean, yes, probably." Should I admit to being bad in bed? Wasn't that like turning myself in for a crime I'd never gotten the chance to commit? Or robbing myself at gunpoint and giving the money to a bank?

"I want us to get off on the right foot," I said. "Or feet. I'm not *mostly vegan*. Or even vegetarian. I only eat meat once every week or two. But it's not important to me as, you know, a thing."

Her back straightened. "Why did you lie then?"

"I exaggerated."

"You lied. Why?"

She was overreacting, wasn't she? "*Lie* is a pretty strong word." I liked truth fine enough, but in a battle to the death with story, I'd cheer for story every time. "You looked like a vegetarian," I said.

"*Pff*. How does someone *look* like a vegetarian? Was I wearing a tofu hat?"

"Well... are you a vegetarian?"

Her voice quietened. "Yes."

"Ha! Told you!"

"Lucky guess." She broke eye contact. "I don't like lies."

"Who likes lies? That's not a thing. No one wakes up and says, 'Do you know what I'd really fancy today? Double deception with a side of falsehood, please.'"

"No, I meant I've had really bad..."

Our feet brushed under the table. I left mine resting against hers. She looked down. "I feel like we should..." She weighed her words, checking their heft. "Before it gets... I'm not... you know... looking for anything right now."

Was I that see-through? "And what makes you think I am?"

"What makes you think I think you are?"

"Why else would you bring it up?"

"You're a man. I'm a woman. We'll spend a lot of time together."

I was a toddler in a man suit but happy she'd not noticed. She dropped her hands to her lap. "I don't like complicated. I'm not complicated."

"Neither am I."

"Okay."

"Fine," she said.

"Perfect then."

"*Good*."

They called our flight.

# 9

# THE FIRST DRIVE: TRIVANDRUM CENTRAL RAILWAY STATION

"That's it!" I said, pointing at the enormous grey slab of a building coming up fast on our left, four lanes of jostling traffic away: Trivandrum Station. Somehow, more by luck than Evelyn's judgement, we had survived the roundabout.

"I don't know if I can."

"You can." I scooted to the left of the tuk-tuk, scrunched my metaphorical ignorance card into my hand, stuck my arms out of the tuk-tuk, and waved them up and down.

*We're coming!*

*We're coming through!*

"After this one, GO!" The tuk-tuk angled left. "More. Turn! More!"

"Wait for this bus. NOW!" We crossed another lane. We screeched through the entrance and met the acquaintance of yet another—much smaller—roundabout.

She'd only stalled six times on the way.

"We didn't die!" she said, as we completed our first lap. "That's so great," she added, at the end of the second rotation. "Wheeeeeee," she said, at the end of the third. "This is fun."

"I feel drunk."

"It's like a carousel."

"Evelyn."

"Yes?"

"Park before I throw up."

"Oh. Okay. Where?"

The station was full to the brim with humans trampling paths and flowerbeds; schlepping suitcases; hugging family members; and being corralled by men in luminous jackets. I pointed to a slither of space near the wide entranceway.

"How am I going to fit? Do we have reverse?"

"Reverse? *Hmm*. No one's mentioned it. I can push us in."

She rolled past the space and I hopped out, grabbed the tuk-tuk's frame, and tugged it backwards. A man in a shiny yellow jacket appeared. Seeing Evelyn in the driver's seat made him hyperventilate.

"Hello, sir," I said, as he moved closer. "Wanna help pull?"

"What?" he wheezed. "Doing?"

"Parking."

"No park here!"

"Just for a minute? I only need a platform ticket."

I kept pulling. I'm a staunch believer in the bendability of rules. Not universally, but for me. Confidence is humanity's killer feature, and I was good at projecting it. And what kind of rule is no parking? One of the minor ones, for sure. A keep off the grass, don't feed the ducks, *I* before *E* except after *C* kind of rule.

And this was India.

And I was white.

And wearing a lanyard.

And smiling.

And we were in a brightly painted tuk-tuk being inexpertly driven by a blonde woman (even if the colour came mostly from a bottle).

We had *make an exception* written all over us.

"No."

"What?"

"No."

"Please?" I kept pulling anyway. We'd almost parked now. He blew his whistle, and— more surprised than annoyed—I stopped. I had overestimated the worth of my privilege.

Evelyn rolled her tongue across her teeth. "New plan. You run for the ticket and I'll keep driving around the roundabout until you get back?"

"I like the way you think," I said, skipping past Mr No and into the station.

Inside, I came face-to-face with an epic hullabaloo of Indian queueing. As a Brit, even if there were nothing to queue for, and I were sitting alone in the middle of an empty field, and it were the end of the world, and I were the only person left alive, I'd still be queueing in my mind.

But this was not Britain. Indians don't appreciate the first-come-first-served nature of Western queueing. This is a collectivist society. Their approach to the queue is fluid and involves surrounding whatever they want and pushing their will upon it as a loose, jazzy mass.

It's not an efficient solution. It's perhaps not even a solution. But they're committed to it.

Before this formless clutter of humans were fifteen windows. I went to the nearest one. It was being mobbed by people so keen to show their purchase intent that they had their money out and up, waving it above their heads, foisting it towards a harried-looking man sitting behind the glass screen, pecking at a computer keyboard. When he surfaced from his device, I made eye contact, utilising my dual advantages of height and foreignness.

"Platform ticket?" I shouted.

He held up two fingers. "Window two."

Window two was the only empty window. Exactly how I liked my windows. Few people wanted a ticket to go almost nowhere.

In less than five minutes, I was back outside and in proud possession of this knick-knack of bureaucracy. But the station roundabout was conspicuously Evelyn-less. A new security operative was there, however. In other countries he would have been keeping the peace, but in India this was an absurd suggestion. At best, he was here to minimise the disorder.

"Seen a white girl in a tuk-tuk?"

"White girl tuk-tuk?"

"Looks like a young Bette Midler?" This didn't help. "No?" I shrugged. "Me neither."

A tuk-tuk turned into the station, looped the roundabout twice, clipped the curb, narrowly avoided the outstretched paws of a snoozing dog, and then stuttered to a stop before us. Together, the security operative and I appraised the curious woman in it. Her wide eyes, tightly closed mouth, and pronounced forehead creasing suggested that she was being held hostage by herself.

"People kept whistling at me," she said.

The man put his yellow whistle in his mouth and blew.

"See?"

"No stop."

"I was just driving around the roundabout, minding my own business, singing eighties power ballads to myself, getting a bit dizzy maybe, sure, but then people were whistling at me and someone honked and I thought I'd go round the block instead but then it didn't end and then more people honked and whistled and I think I'm done and I hate this and I want to kill myself or go home or both."

The man whistled again.

"See?"

"No stop."

She'd been brave going out into traffic knowing that if she stalled, she'd be stuck. "Shall I take over?"

"No."

"I don't mind."

"*No.*"

I squashed into the back and we edged out of the station, hanging the tuk-tuk's nose into the passing stream of traffic. No space came. That's not how it works here. Space is not given, it's taken. I thought about telling Evelyn this, encouraging her out, but she knew it already, had her own approach to dealing with it. One different from my own, it seemed. More measured, thoughtful, nuanced, dizzying.

I scooted across the seat to the right and waved my arms about. It was something I could do. Something she couldn't stop me from doing. Inch by inch, nudge by nudge, she created a gap that, just as slowly, we filled.

At the next junction, we found a tuk-tuk driver who both knew our hotel and agreed to lead us to it. At its entrance, Aarav stood waving a chequered flag.

"Better late than never," he yelled, as we passed.

In the car park stood twenty-one of the no-longer-gleaming tuk-tuks.

Evelyn turned off the engine as relief flooded through me. "We did it," I whispered.

"If you'd known what *it* would be like, would you still have come?"

"No," I said, without hesitation.

"I'm..." She stopped. "Do you think we'll make it?"

I rubbed at the sides of my head. A runaway-mine-train of a headache was roaring through. "No."

10

# BACK TO OUR ARRIVAL IN TRIVANDRUM

*HONK, HONK, HONK*

The tuk-tuk driver contributed three mechanical burps to the soundtrack of frustration blaring around us as we inched our way from the airport into Trivandrum's centre. He had places to go, damn it. Who did all these people think they were?

On *his* road.

In *his* way.

*HONK, HONK, HONK*

He hit them again. Hit them where it hurt. Hit them right in the kisser. That would show them. Put them in their place. Let them know he was not a man whose time could be so brazenly trifled with.

*HONK, HONK, HOOOOONK*

I inhaled, and a blast of cardamom, incense, petrol, and sewage thudded up into my skull. The humidity was as thick as day-old soup.

I'd been to India just once before, a decade earlier, and had never forgotten the sharpness of its bite. I'd always planned to write about it before the memories faded. I'd tried often, stretching out at my desk before a line of photos, cracking my knuckles, dropping my fingers to the keys, jogging out a brisk sentence or two, only to collapse, coughing and spluttering, before the paragraph mark. It was even an exhausting place to describe; a marathon of a culture to run as you pulled people along behind in a chariot of words, pointing out all the incredible sights and views and weirdness appearing on the left and right.

India is everything good about humanity throwing a raucous, several-thousand-year-long party for everything that's bad.

It was great to be back. To be hunkered next to Evelyn in the backseat of the most common sight on an Indian road: a black-and-yellow tuk-tuk taxi—one of a swarm of mechanical bees pincering tourists and buzzing them through maddening, logic-defying traffic to different petals in its flower.

"Traffic bad today," I said to our driver, an Indian Burt Reynolds lookalike. He glanced in the rearview mirror, and his head undulated on his neck in a nod that kept slipping on its way down: the Indian *hewobble*.

Another thing I'd missed. While it just means *yes*, I've always felt it hints at more, gestures to the duality of all things —that true is false false, up is inverted down, one person's terrorist is another's freedom fighter, and reality will always be obfuscated by the black box behind our eyes.

I shooed a flower seller away only for a boy holding a tray stacked with plastic torches to take her place. Why would we need a torch? A woman holding a purple bucket of water bottles elbowed him aside. Water was logical, at least. The heat wrapped us up as if we were mummies. A newspaper seller quickly trampled her in an aggressive duet with a toothless hawker of chewing gum. Street capitalism's tide was coming in, splashing us with all these things we didn't need, while over on the cracked pavement, people took part in an intricate, frenetic, swirling dance of practised civility.

I put my head in my hands. It was already too much—visual music played at such a loud volume I couldn't hear myself think.

Evelyn tapped out an e-mail on her phone.

"You work too much."

She frowned. "Do I?"

The journey had given us ample time to put on our overalls and hard hats and mine each other. From her rock face, I'd excavated the following lumps of fact: she ran the press office of a left-wing political party; had at least two funny anecdotes on any topic; knew the names of several types of wine; had been (non-ironically) to the opera; was prone to winking; and was overly reasonable about everyone else and too hard on herself.

The more pieces of her I picked up, dusted off, and held to the light, the more certain I became that I wanted but would never have her. It was the opposite of "Breakfast in France."

She slipped her phone into her brown leather handbag. "In your books, how much is true?"

"I don't like that question."

"Then it's probably a good one, no?"

"I don't know. The framing is wrong, somehow."

"Why?"

"Well, let's say in two years, if we still know each other, that I ask you about this conversation."

"I'll remember it."

"You think you will, yeah."

*HONK, HONK, HONK*

"I've an excellent memory." She picked some fluff from her denim shirt. "Women are usually the keepers of memories." She waited for me to challenge this, then continued when I didn't. "Maybe they have less forgetting luxury?" She often translated from German, which resulted in some creative nouning. German is all about the nouns in the same way Imelda Marcos was all about the shoes.

"So, you'll remember what we said? The specifics, I mean?"

She lifted her chin. "Maybe not the specifics. But broadly, yes."

"You won't, but let's pretend you will. Now you need to tell the story of this conversation."

Her eyes moved in a slow circle. "I could do that."

*HONK, HONK, HONK*

"But you can't tell it broadly, right? Because people want to be in this moment with us. They want to sit on our shoulders, looking conspiratorially out at the world as we do *right now*. You can't say, 'And then in the tuk-tuk we had a bit of a chat about truth and how Evelyn works too hard.'"

"That doesn't mean you can just make stuff up though." She straightened. "The truth matters." *Ah, the truth again.*

"I don't. I know the broad strokes: the emotions, the sentiments, what a ride in a taxi in India is like, how this conversation informs the next, and so on."

"But then it's not true."

"It's true to the spirit."

"Yeah." She winked. "That sounds like a cop out."

"Calling something a cop out is a cop out. Memory is rubbish. Everything is random. History is written by the victor. You're your own victor, remembering it how you need it to be."

A light flicked on behind her eyes. "Winston Churchill."

"What about him?"

"'History is written by the victor.'"

"What? I thought I just came up with that?"

She laughed. "No."

"I was proud of that line."

"He probably was too."

"But..." My face twisted. "I mean... couldn't I *also* have come up with it, though? *Independently*?"

"Independently, you say?"

"Yes."

"Maybe you should pitch a movie to Hollywood in which aliens attack earth but we're saved by Will Smith. You could call it *Independently Day*."

It was really hard not to laugh at this, but I couldn't let her win. "That's... that's... *timeism*! You're totally, massively *timeist*! You're discriminating against me!"

Her tongue poked through her teeth. "Discrimination, you say? Western European heterosexual white man?"

"Yes!"

"Oh, this should be good..."

"You're *timeist*! It's like racism but for time."

"I got that."

"I'm being unfairly victimised."

"You don't need to say *unfairly* before you say victimised. No one is fairly victimised."

"What about murderers?"

"You think they victimise murderers?"

She'd trapped me. "Don't distract me!"

"Carry on."

"You're totally, massively *timeist*! You discriminate against great thinkers like me just because we have the misfortune to be born late, after all the good ideas and snappy retorts have already been taken."

She coughed. "Great thinkers?"

"Yeah. I think..." A small amount of doubt slipped in through an open window. "I think... *that I think*... that I came up with that 'history is written by the victor' line on my own."

She cocked an eyebrow. "Yeah, well, I think *that I think* that you didn't. And also, we've got indoor plumbing now, and you won't die from an infected tooth. So, it's not all bad in the present, is it?"

I looked away before she could shoot me with any more bullets of cold, hard reasoning.

Up ahead, a bus vomited humans onto the pavement. Its doors closed, and it inched forwards just enough to entice our driver to swerve around it and speed into a tiny gap between a gas truck and an exquisitely filthy lorry. How had he missed both?

Tomorrow, this would be us: rolling out on three wheels into this cluster fudge of humans, machines, and, sometimes, even cows.

"It can't be that hard, right?" I said. Evelyn's eyes met mine, and I urged them towards our driver.

"Keep telling yourself that."

A heavy, immovable stone of dread sat in the pit of my stomach.

A few minutes and double-digit horn honks later, we came to a stop outside a large glass-fronted dome, almost exactly like the spaceship in *Independence Day* and the spaceship I also planned, independently, to use in *Independently Day*.

I peered out at it. "This looks fancy."

"It better be. I'm too old for bucket showers."

"How old are you?" Somehow the question had never come up.

"Thirty-four."

"Me too." It was just another sign of how fated and destined for an epic Happy Ever After we were.

She paid the driver. I leaned down to grab her backpack, but she slapped my arm away and hoisted it up onto her back. The dome's electric doors parted.

We had arrived.

11

# LATER THAT DAY: OUR FIRST EVENING IN INDIA

Jet lag was a small, tenacious dog nipping at me. I squished deeper into the duvet, savouring the thought that it would be a full week before I'd have to go back to that dreaded demon place, that bane of every traveller's life: Securityland. Where we're reduced to human cattle. Where we're stripped, patted, scanned, stamped, tagged, and prodded in pens guarded by armed uniforms trying to convince us of the impossible: that we're safe and that all this aggressive, inconvenient tomfoolery is in our best interests.

The hotel was booked out with tuk-tuk racers, so we had to share Evelyn's twin room, accommodation booked as part of the race package. I'd tried to hide my excitement at this but felt it had leaked out at the edges of my body language, at the slight spring in my step.

I looked over at her open black suitcase. There were the things of *her*—a red bra, a straw hat, a faded blue T-shirt. If I knew the things, I'd better understand the whole, and then I could better seduce it.

But I was very tired. I'd start the seduction tomorrow.

*How long until we can sleep?* I checked my phone: it was

only late afternoon. To slip smoothly into our new time zone, we'd need to keep our eyes open quite a while longer yet.

Evelyn returned from the bathroom, removed the wet towel from her head, and dumped it onto her bed.

"Do you know anywhere for dinner?" I asked.

"Usually I do my research," she said, attacking the wild knots in her hair with a wand comb the size of Calcutta. It got stuck immediately. She looked like someone trying to tame the Amazon with a robot vacuum cleaner. "I hate wasting calories. But I was busy, and since all the food here is amazing anyway, especially for vegetarians like me and"—she gave an ironic mini-cough—"*you*..."

"How long before you let that go?"

"A bit longer yet."

Giving up on her hair, she threw it into a chunky ponytail, and then we wandered down past reception to electric doors that parted. A whoosh of humidity slapped us in the face, and we stepped out into Trivandrum.

In the average Indian city, the untrained and unforgiving eye might find little that appeals. In fact, those of a harsh and critical nature might conclude they're just loud, polluted, gridlocked urban hellholes—places where extraordinary numbers of people hunch together in what they've been told is a vehicle of prosperity but looks more like a joyride off an urban cliff in a free-market bus with no brakes. This was what made Trivandrum, Kerala's capital, such a pleasant surprise. Home to just a million people, it was a lively, but ordered city. It wore a green cloak over its hilly shoulders. Its roads were full but whisking white-collar workers to and from technology parks before a backdrop of traditional sloping red-tile roofs and squat modern malls drenched in the shrill, neon promises of phone companies and clothing brands.

Kerala is one of India's shining stars and widely regarded as its best place to live. It's a state that outperforms the US on many metrics, has India's second-lowest corruption rate and highest literacy rate, and places a progressive 14.5% "fat tax" on certain junk foods.

A few streets from the hotel, already wheezing from the heat, we stopped in a square to buy water and get our bearings. As we did, a short man approached us. He was bow-legged and shuffled as though carrying a heavy barrel.

"Nice t-shirtttt," he said to me, with an enthusiastic thumbs up.

I looked down to see what T-shirt I was wearing: it was plain and grey. "Err, thanks."

He wore a striped black-and-silver shirt that was misbuttoned. On his head sat a dome of fluffy brown hair that looked like a mushroom hat. He hovered, grinning, neither making conversation nor forbidding it.

"Do you know a nice restaurant around here?" I asked.

"Surrrre. What are you looking forrr?" His speech crept like a prowler through the bushes of the night.

"Whatever's popular," Evelyn said. "Needn't be fancy. But if it's fancy, that's also okay, I suppose. You just live once, right? Oh wait, not here. I'm babbling."

He plunged his hands into the pockets of his scuffed jeans. "There's a pllllace nearby." His eyes were bloodshot. "I can shhhhhow you, if you waaaant?"

"Okay," I said. "You hungry?"

"Always, my brother." He looked at Evelyn. "And sister."

"We'll invite you then," I said, ushering him down the road.

"Adam."

"Toby."

"Evelyn."

Hands were shaken but not stirred.

"Where's your hotel?" he asked.

"Oh, it's nearby," Evelyn said.

"The Hyacinth?"

"No."

"Central Residency?"

"No." I wondered why she wasn't telling him the name. I'd forgotten the name.

"The Royal Heritage?"

"No." Each no doubled in size.

"Which road?"

"It's that way." She pointed far from where my mental map had it situated. My mental map is legendary. While I never know where I am, or the name of where I'm going, or that of where I've come from, I move between them masterfully.

Evelyn stepped closer to me and whispered in German, "Why does he care so much where we're staying?"

"Just being friendly." I switched back to English. "*Toby*? That doesn't sound like an Indian name."

"It's my Western name."

"Why do you need a Western name?"

He shrugged. "It's eeeeeasier."

He led us down an alley so narrow I could have reached out and touched the buildings on either side. A loose power cable crackled overhead as we turned sideward to shimmy past a blue bin. On it, a split bag of rubbish leaked a mysterious black ooze. Inside the bin, a rat squeaked.

"Just a bit further," Toby said, stopping outside an open door. A door so open, in fact, it had jumped its hinges entirely. The restaurant behind it was an empty, dark hovel.

I paused in the doorway. Travelling is always a negotiation between the known, the unknown, and the unknowable.

I *knew* that if you're not sure where to eat, eat somewhere busy, where the food is most likely to be fresh.

I *knew* it would be hard to criticise this establishment without criticising Toby.

*Unknown* was why, of all the thousands of restaurants in this city, he'd picked this one.

*Unknowable* was whether, if we agreed to eat here, we'd get very, very sick. For my stomach is as weak as my mental map is legendary. Inside, Toby climbed a rickety, wooden staircase that lifted us to a narrow mezzanine level built for people of Toby's height, not mine. He plonked himself in the booth furthest from the entrance. "Good food."

I tried to slide in opposite him, but my shorts stuck firm on a patch of grime. I ripped myself free. Evelyn sat next to me, moving gingerly, as if the place were made of dynamite and one wrong step would cause it to explode beneath her. She sat and fingered the bottom edge of her black shirt, which was covered in tiny leopards. Toby tried to keep his eyes from falling on her chest. He was unsuccessful.

A dozen flies, elated at having someone to irritate, irritated. This was what they'd trained for.

"I'll just see if the chef is awake," he said, heading for the stairs.

"Awake?" whispered Evelyn. "It's 6pm." She looked around. "This place is..." She wanted to criticise it, but her impeccable middle-class upbringing didn't allow for it. "I don't want to get sick. Not on day one."

"He's a local, though."

"So?"

"I'm sure he knows what he's doing."

He disappeared through swing doors into the kitchen. "Is there something about him, maybe?" she said. "A kind of vibe?"

"He's a nice guy," I said. "Just a bit stoned."

"You're just saying that because he liked your T-shirt."

"It's a nice T-shirt."

"It's grey."

"Grey's a good colour."

"Yeah, for maximising anonymity."

She swept the restaurant with her eyes before realising it was far too dirty for just one sweep. And so, she swept it again. "I had an old roommate in Israel. Gemma," she said. I settled in for another Evelyn story. "English girl. Drank too much. Incredible breasts. Anyway, she came to India in the early 2000s with a friend. They got in a taxi at the airport and give the driver the hotel's address. He looks at it, scratches his head, looks at it more, frowns. 'This can't be right because this hotel has closed down.'

"'But we just booked it,' they said. He got out his phone and called the number. No answer. The number was disconnected. Weird, right?"

"Classic scam," I said.

"Anyway, he said he knows a good hotel, a fine hotel, good price for them. His brother's hotel. He takes them there. On the way they stop at a restaurant he recommends. The new hotel is horrible but they're too tired to find a new one. And they don't know where they are. And they're not feeling good."

"Everyone gets sick in India at some point."

"First meal? Anyway, they wake up and guess who's there? Their friendly driver."

"Probably visiting his brother?"

"Yeah. Only when they asked the owner, he said all his brothers lived in the north."

"Weird."

"Yeah. The taxi driver brings them medicine and comes to visit them each day with food and water. Once they're better, he appoints himself as their personal driver. Although they said he was more like a personal assistant. Insisted on buying everything for them because he said he'd get it cheaper."

"That might be true."

"Yeah, except on the last day they did a test. While he was

in the toilet, they went to the shop he'd just gone to for them. I can't remember what he bought—shampoo, let's say. They found out he'd doubled the cost."

"Come on, that India is long gone. We've both been here before and it's fine."

"Yeah. But I was with my Indian friend last time, so nothing happened."

*A male friend? Just a friend? Why were we not meeting him on this trip? Why wasn't he racing with us?*

So many questions, almost all of them the irrational ravings of an insecure, jealous man in a fantastic grey T-shirt drowning in a poisonous pond of Doubt.

"Nothing happened to me last time I was here," I said. "And I was alone. Well, a few things happened: minor scams and wrong bills. We're just going to have a nice meal with our new, dopey friend and then go back to the hotel."

"Yeah, or he's a poisoner! Why was he so interested in where we're staying? Just because you're paranoid doesn't mean people aren't out to get... I mean... *poison* you." She unstuck the menu from the tabletop and wiped the grime off it with a tissue. The sound of crashing pots thundered out from the kitchen.

"He just woke up," Toby said on his return. "But it's ffffine."

"Very quiet here?" I said, because even if it's obvious, that doesn't mean you shouldn't state it.

"Yeah. Early."

I nodded. "Toby, I'm sure it's great here, but do you perhaps know somewhere busier?"

His bloodshot eyes widened. "You don't like this place?"

"It's... got a lot going for it. *Really*. But perhaps there's somewhere with more... *ehm*... people-watching opportunities?"

"The chef is my brother."

"And we're sure"—I opened my palms to Evelyn, who was mid-squirm—"aren't we, Evelyn, that he's excellent at what he does."

By which I meant sleeping and banging pots.

"You don't want to eat here though?" He crossed his arms. "I guess we could go somewhere else."

We leapt up from our seats as much as was possible under the circumstances.

"You don't want to say goodbye to your brother?" I asked, as we reached the doorway. He turned back towards the kitchen. "No, it's fine."

We retraced our steps down the alley of doom before Toby led us to a pleasant street-front restaurant that bustled with a dozen customers being served by sixty-seven enthusiastic staff members in crisp white uniforms.

A waiter arrived.

"Can I get a whisky?" Toby asked.

"Sure," Evelyn said, before I could object. I wasn't suspicious, but I was frugal. And we were already buying him dinner.

The whisky arrived. Toby drank it like a shot, then licked his lips. "Delicious."

We checked the menu. It was clean, and the food sounded appetising. "So, do you think maybe I could get another whisky?" he asked.

In the distance I heard the clang of bells. Alarm bells. Evelyn continued to squirm in her seat, avoiding eye contact with us both.

"Erm. So…" I chewed the lumps out of my words. "Toby, we're not drinking tonight. But we'll happily buy you dinner. And that first whisky. Okay?"

He wafted his hand towards me with so much nonchalance it was as if everything I'd said was his idea. "Sure… You're going to Goa?"

We nodded.

"Yeah, everyone loves Goa, man. You can party. Drink. Drugs. Sex. Do you like drugs?"

"Sure," said Evelyn.

*Does Evelyn take drugs? What drugs? Does she get them from men? What men?*

She didn't seem the drug type. Although whisky is a drug, I guess. Coffee is a drug. Lust is a drug. I was getting very, very high just looking at her. Everything we do changes everything we are. *Drug* is a mostly meaningless word.

"Yeah," he continued. "Goa is not like Trivandrum, brother. Goa is party, party, party. Party on the beach. Party by the beach. Party... man. In Goa you're free. Free to do what you want. Free to *paaaaaarty*."

He was like a Beastie Boys song bought to life.

"You seem to like Goa a lot?"

"Yeah, man. I'm from Goa."

"Whereabouts?"

"Just Goa."

"It's big though, no?"

"Yeah."

"Why do you live in Trivandrum?" Evelyn asked.

"University."

I relaxed. He was a learned person. A scholar. A man of letters. "Which university?"

"Oh, you know, the main one." *And vagaries.*

"What are you studying?"

"Economics." He pushed out his lips. "Like the economy and stuff. Money. I like money."

"I studied that too," I said. Evelyn squinted. She knew what I'd studied. We'd discussed it on the plane. "Sort of," I added, to appease her strong desire for truth. I'd studied business, but there'd been a few modules on economics, and I prided myself on having a minute of class-A anecdotes on every topic.

"What are you studying in particular?"

"Just about the moneys and stuff. The economy."

"Who's your favourite economist?"

"I like them all, really."

Suspicion grew like weeds in my garden of disbelief. "Is the Indian economy well run, do you think? Is it Keynesian?"

I didn't remember exactly what Keynesian economics was, just that it believed in interventions during recessions.

"Yeah, man. Kenyan." To my knowledge, Kenyan economics was not a thing outside Kenya.

Evelyn sucked at the second half of her mango lassi. I'd yet to find a drink she couldn't defeat in under a minute of enthusiastic slurping. "I went on a date with a venture capitalist once," she said. "Very nice hair. By the end of the first drink"—*After sixty seconds, in her case*—"I knew it could never work. It's the only time I've felt that on a date. And I've been on a lot of dates. Why would you give your life to money?"

*Why has she been on so many dates? She's perfect. Is she also picky? Oh no.*

She was happiest when she had a story to offer. She had a very Keynesian approach to awkwardness, believed in tackling it head-on with a swift interventionist anecdote policy, no matter how irrelevant. It seemed as if she scanned conversations for keywords and when she got a match, her shoulders relaxed, knowing the next minutes were hers alone, free of the dance of actual conversation and the possibility people would stand on her sentences' feet.

I didn't mind. She told stories well.

"Yeah, money is good," said Toby, missing the point of this one entirely.

"I read a book about the informal economy here," she

continued. "About gangs in slums. And how few jobs here are regulated and pay tax. It's like an 80-percent-informal economy, right?"

"Tax?" Toby handled the word like Sisyphus his boulder. "Tax sucks, brother."

Not a nuanced position for an economist. You can't run an economy on love. He looked to Evelyn but not her eyes. "And sister."

Evelyn simultaneously lowered her head and raised her eyes towards me in a classic pose of the I-told-you-so genre.

"Do you have to do a dissertation?" I asked.

"What's that?"

"The big paper you write last."

"Yeeeeah. I'm doing that now."

"What's yours on?"

"Just like the moneys and stuff."

"What about the moneys and stuff, specifically?"

"How you can, *like*, get more of it?"

I wasn't sure why this had been stated as a question.

"So, I have this money tree," he said. "I collect money from around the world. Different notes, you know?"

"Uh-huh." I was having fun now. Looking forward to where this was going. How it might end. The story it might become.

"Do you maybe have, like, a note for me?" he asked innocently.

"What currency?"

"Any."

"Any," I said, in mock surprise. "But isn't it a collection?"

"Yeah. *A collection*."

Evelyn appeared to be desperately scouring her mind for another relevant-but-benign anecdote. Did she have anything on trees? On money? On collections? She reminded me of how I'd been when we first met, as I was trying to lasso her into a conversation.

"I went on a date with a man who collected stamps," she said, having got a hit in her story search engine. "Stamps—can you believe that? I mean. Odd. Of all the beauty and weirdness, you pick stamps? Tells you a lot about a person, I think." She signalled for another lassi. "Stamps, you know?"

Her Story Tourette's was strong today. I sharpened my tone. "Evelyn."

"*Sorry.*"

"Isn't it important to know if you have that currency already? Otherwise you'll double it, no?"

"Yeah, brother." He looked to Evelyn. "And sister."

"I bet you have the euro already, right? That's very common."

"Euro." He let the word roam. "No, I don't have a euro note."

"Weird."

"I know. Do you perhaps have a euro note for meeeeee?"

I pretended to think it over. "Sorry," I said. "We're all out."

Evelyn's cheeks had broken out into a rash. Was she allergic to awkwardness? Why did it affect her so strongly?

"A coin, then?" he asked.

"You have space for coins on your tree?"

"Yeah, sure."

"How are they attached?"

"Attached?"

"Like with tape?"

"Yeah, with tape."

"Single-sided or double?"

"Yeah, tape."

Evelyn gripped the table's edge.

"It's okay, Toby," I said. "*Brother*. You don't have to lie.

You're a con artist, not an economist."

His eyes squirmed in their sockets. "No. Brother."

"We're not annoyed. It's fine. Fun, even. Can we just have a nice dinner then go our separate ways?"

"I'm not lying."

"You are. It's fine."

The food arrived. We tore into it, making only occasional eye contact.

"I had a bad week," he said, halfway through his kozhi: a coriander-, chilli-, and onion-heavy chicken dish that released wafts of spicy heaven. Did I say heaven? Sorry, I meant hell. I'm a vegetarian, remember. Mostly.

"I had, like, my money for rent, at the university," he said. "Where, you know, I study. At the university, you know? Economics. So, the money for one month's rent. I had it in my pocket."

"Just loose in your pocket?"

"Yeah. Then I lost it somehow."

I let my fork clatter onto the plate. "Oh no. *Oh no.*" I clamped my eyes shut. "*Oh no no no no no no no.*"

"*Yeah.* It must have fallen out somewhere?"

"Just fell out?"

"Yeah."

"Terrible. Just terrible."

"Yeah. Just fell out, I guess."

"You didn't put it in a wallet?"

I tried to meet Evelyn's eyes, but she'd fixed them to the exit.

"No. Just loose."

"Just loose."

"*Just loose.*"

I pinched the bridge of my nose. "Awful."

"And the dorm supervisor said if I don't pay tonight, he'll kick me out!"

"By tonight?" There wasn't much tonight left. Which was the good news. Because, sleep.

"Yeah."

"You'll be homeless?"

"Uh-huh."

"Less a home?"

"Uh-huh." My sarcasm was failing to penetrate.

"On the street."

"Yep."

"Just you and your money tree."

"Yep."

Evelyn signalled for the bill while still chewing her last mouthful of food.

"So," Toby said. "I was wondering, maybe, if you could, like, lend me some money? Because I lost it. You know? It fell out of my pocket."

"Just out of your pocket?"

"Yeah."

"Terrible. How much do you need?"

He rubbed the back of his neck. "Like a hundred euros? But, I mean, anything would help."

I raised my hands. "Stop, Toby."

"Stop what?"

"You're a con artist. It's fine. I respect it, even. Takes some real chutzpah. I'd love to talk about it. How did you get started? How much do you earn a week? Does that money tree story ever work?"

He clicked his jaw. "I have a money tree."

"You don't."

"And my rent." He sighed theatrically. "I mean, anything would help."

"Toby. *Stop*. It's okay. Please. Just break character."

"No character, brother, man." He looked at Evelyn. "*Sister*. It's my life!"

"Yeah... but it's not though, is it?"

Evelyn was now the colour of a ripe tomato. She paid the bill and strode ahead onto the street, going the wrong direction, away from the hotel. Or so I thought. *Wait, where's the...? Did someone move our hotel?*

"I guess they'll kick me out then," Toby said, falling into step with me.

"Uh-huh."

"Homeless."

"Less a home."

"Can I walk you back?"

"No."

"Want to get a whisky? My brother owns a place."

"Isn't he a chef?"

His eyes swept the space ahead of him like searchlights. "Different brother."

"Toby." I stopped and puffed out my chest.

"Yeah."

"*Go away.*"

I turned and jogged to catch up with Evelyn. Toby trailed a few metres behind us, so we quickened our pace and darted into a small shopping mall where, bravely, we hid behind a display of brightly coloured saris until he left.

"Oh, my God," Evelyn said, flapping her hand in front of her face. "That was awful. So, so awful. Incredibly awkward. Why did you do that?"

"Do what?"

"Make it so awkward?"

"Was it? Did I? *Oh*. I thought it was fun."

"I can't handle awkwardness."

"I'm starting to notice. I quite like it. It's a sign you don't know what will happen next."

"I'm not sure why that's a good thing. And you didn't need to be rude."

"I was rude?"

"Yes."

"Huh. I got annoyed, I guess?"

"Still, you can't just confront people like that."

"He was trying to trick us, though. What would you have done?"

"Well, I wouldn't have invited him for dinner. As a woman you have to be more careful. And I'm bad at..."

"Saying no?"

"Yeah. We didn't do confrontation in our family. Well, my dad did, but just by screaming and throwing things."

She shook out her arms. Her anger was dissipating either because I wasn't screaming and throwing things or because she was trying to avoid awkwardness by pushing down her feelings. We buried the topic, sat on a bench, and watched the surrounding shops surrender hope of further trade and close their shutters for the night.

"It was all a scam, right?" I said.

She nodded. "Every word."

A tall, skinny man approached us. I'd forgotten how often people approached foreigners here, or simply stared. "Hey, friend," the man said. "Where you from?"

"Hey," I said flatly. "Germany."

"Germany!" He looked down at my clothes. "Nice T-shirt."

Evelyn and I laughed.

"You're on holiday?"

"Yeah, kind of." I remembered the real reason we were here: the race. It was like being dunked headfirst in an icy plunge pool.

"So, I was wondering... I have this money tree where I collect notes from around the world. Just small—"

"Do you know Toby by any chance?" Evelyn asked.

"Toby?" His eyes widened. "Yeah, he's my brother!"

12

## KOVALAM BEACH

Evelyn looked out at the tuk-tuks scattered like leaves across the hotel's car park. Training day was over and our time in the school's playground had left us hobbled, humbled, and bleeding from a dozen wounds in our hands. A toll had been taken, and we had an afternoon and evening of recreation to steal it back.

Or so we'd thought. Sitting together in the hotel's restaurant, one by one, each team of petrol sadists announced they would take their tuk-tuks back out for further practice, pointing their bumpers towards Kovalam Beach, some thirty minutes' drive from the hotel, on the outskirts of the city.

It was the worst idea since the mullet.

"Should we go too?" Evelyn asked. "It would make sense. But then we're here, and this makes no sense, so maybe we're not very sensical?"

"Do you want to?" I said, stirring the lumps from my pineapple smoothie.

She sucked in her cheeks. "As much as I want to have bricks thrown at me. Can we drink yet? I'm stressed."

I didn't want more stress. I wanted soft music, furnishings, and cheeses. But our not practicing didn't bode well for our chances of winning the race, a goal we'd not discussed as a possibility because it was so absurd. We'd also not discussed how much better—although stickier—the world would be if it were made of pineapple lassi.

"How about we take a normal taxi to the beach?" she asked.

We were less than a metre from the hotel's entrance before the first tuk-tuk taxi dive-bombed us. Getting a taxi here didn't require proactivity, merely the absence of resistance.

"How much to Kovalam Beach?" Evelyn asked.

The driver angled his head towards me. "Five dollars."

"Mmm," she said, with the authority of a chimp in ER scrubs. It wasn't much money, but she knew she should haggle. But then haggling could get awkward, and she couldn't abide the awkward. I could help with that.

"May I?" I asked, in German.

"I can do it."

"I just think he wants to deal with me." I turned to him. "Price not good, sir," I said, blowing the horn on a multi-round, fake-tense price negotiation in which—to keep the taxi driver paranoid—I skilfully played the roles of both Good and Bad Cop, at some points even berating myself.

I was a maverick. A loose cannon. A man on the edge.

But then, suddenly, *reasonable*. What was all this talk of *edge*? I pulled everyone back in, calmed them down, made them tea, and offered them biscuits. It would be fine, now, because *I* was here. Not that other guy. I was everyone's friend. Their ally.

BUT NOT SOMEONE TO CROSS!

It was a lot of fun... for me. We settled on $3.50 and squashed together in the back, where Evelyn avoided making eye contact with me.

"You're annoyed?"

"Why would I be annoyed?"

I rolled my eyes. "That's a classic annoyed person's double-cross sentence."

"I could have handled it just fine. You pushed too hard on the price."

"It was the starting offer. And haggling is fun. And I'm good at it. I could sell Eskimos to snow."

"Do you mean snow to Eskimos?"

"Too easy."

"They don't call them Eskimos anymore. It's offensive."

"Your face is offensive."

She turned away from me. I'd assumed she was used to a British style of banter, in which you throw insults back and forth like a lit firework and what's said is less important than the speed with which it's lobbed.

We rode on in silence I was too tired to try and end. Half an hour later, the tuk-tuk careened around a bend and I slid across the seat into Evelyn. When I recovered, the cityscape had been replaced by a cobalt-blue sky and a wall of shimmering sea. To our left sat a brilliant red-and-white lighthouse resting in a nest of palm trees at the foot of a bay that curved to a beach. A dozen bright fishing boats lay at the water's edge, hulls upright, drying in the sun.

Berlin was suddenly a long way away. Indian cities are fine enough, but to come here for them is to miss the embarrassment of natural riches beyond their borders. We walked the promenade past a dozen restaurants whose sentinels rushed out, menus under their arms. Picking the only restaurant that didn't try to recruit us, Evelyn and I sat side-by-side watching the locals splash in the sleepy ocean's surf. The food arrived, and I got to work on the side salad. Evelyn watched, her head turning like the minute hand of a clock. "Do you eat from *worst* to *best*?"

I stopped. "Doesn't everyone?"

"Most people eat from best to worst. I mean, what if you're full by the time you get to the best stuff?"

"Bad luck, I guess?"

"It's an odd system."

"I'm an odd person?"

"No, you're not. You're pretty reasonable."

*Do women want reasonable men? No, reasonableness is a vanilla character trait. Women want men who drive them wild with desire and can wrestle bears shirtless. Vladimir Putin types, one who undemocratically rule warm places with easy access to piña coladas. Like Hawaii, for example.*

"Well." I tried to rationalise my approach. "I like the feeling that the best is still ahead. It used to drive my ex crazy. Peak Theory, she called it."

"I can see why. How long were you together?"

"Eight years, I think. Something like that. How long was your last relationship?"

"What happens when you notice things have peaked?" she said. Another sidestep.

"I want to stop and go do something else."

"How do you know it peaked, though?"

"It's. I don't know. And it was never a big problem because until now, life has consistently been getting better. Your thirties beat your twenties. Your twenties bully your teens. But at some point, it will tip. We'll get old. Our knees will hurt. Our skin will wrinkle. We'll forget things."

"You forget things all the time."

"How dare you."

"What's the name of this beach?"

"K... KK... Kakapo? Coca-Cola Beach?"

"And the name of our hotel?"

I clicked my tongue against my teeth. "Starts with an *A*?"

"It has an *a* in it. Two, actually. And where is it?"

An easy one. No one messed with my mental map. I

pointed in the direction a crow would fly—assuming it had a sense of direction as finely calibrated as mine—to get from our seats to the head of my hotel bed. She laughed, took my arm, and turned it about fifty degrees. She was wrong, but I didn't correct her. It was just another of the many kindnesses I offered as a pretty reasonable man.

"Are you an introvert or an extrovert?" I asked. She'd seemed very confident when we'd met in the bar, but after training day, and how she'd reacted to Toby, I was becoming less sure.

"I read an article about that." This was becoming her catchphrase. "The definition of extroversion is when you get energy from social interactions rather than losing it. I get energy, but it also costs me in other areas. As you've seen. I react strongly to awkwardness."

"REALLY?"

"I think my default stance in life is..." She stopped. She turned towards the ocean. It wasn't clear if more was coming. I waited, enjoying the giggling emanating from nature's water park. She turned back to me. "I don't know if you ever feel this. Imagine you're running late to something. You're leaving the subway. You approach the staircase. You step. You step. You're not thinking about stepping. It's automatic. You've climbed a million staircases." Her voice deepened. "BUT THEN... YOU NOTICE. Notice you're walking up stairs. *Stepping*. How does one walk up stairs? How does one step? The automatic manualises. You stumble. You freeze, one foot in the air."

"I know *exactly* what you mean."

"That moment. That specific moment. That's how I feel at all times."

"Oh, come on. That's not how I experience you at all. And your job?"

"I know."

She wasn't on holiday; she was working somewhere warmer; still coordinating, talking to journalists, smoothing wrangles in communication. It seemed odd to me that someone who hated dependence in one direction seemed to cultivate it in the other. I wanted to ask about it, but I sensed she didn't know the answer. Just as I didn't know why I ate from worst to best. We're puzzles to ourselves as much as to each other.

On the way back to the hotel, I watched our tuk-tuk driver fastidiously, trying to guess when he'd change gears. He was a good driver, which in this part of the world meant he was an aggressive driver. As we neared the train station, we passed the two retired Brits whom I'd crashed into earlier on the hill. They were returning from the beach. Evelyn gave them a huge smile and a thumbs up as our tuk-tuk professional overtook them, sounding his horn in delight.

"Go, old men, go!" He looked back over his shoulder. "Did you see them?"

"Yeah."

"They're driving all the way to Goa. They're crazy."

"Yeah, we're doing it too."

"Racing to Goa" he repeated. "Crazy white people. To Goa!"

"Yeah, we're also racing."

"In a rickshaw!" he clarified, as we passed an all-female American team and the inflatable giraffe they'd strapped to their roof.

"HAAAAAAA!" he screamed, bouncing up and down in his seat, honking the horn. "Women! Driving! Did you see?"

"Yeah." Because we had eyes. "We're doing—"

"To Goa! So far. They will die."

"I know. We're racing too. In a tuk-tuk. I mean rickshaw. With them."

"To Goa. These people are crazy."

Perhaps the idea that we had a tuk-tuk but were paying him to drive us was too absurd to entertain. He had a point.

"Do you want to see all the other rickshaws?" I asked, as we pulled up outside the hotel's reception. If seeing two race tuk-tuks got him this excited, I wanted to see what the sight of twenty more would do.

"Rickshaws?"

"The race. All the rickshaws are here."

"*Here*?"

I walked off towards the car park assuming he'd follow, but when I turned around a few steps later, I saw the back of his tuk-tuk pulling out into the main road. Evelyn was now standing in a circle of Indians at the hotel's entrance. "Where'd that baby come from?" I asked. She tilted the tiny human in her arms towards me as if it were an award she didn't feel she'd earned but would accept. "It just got put there. Cute, right?"

A woman slipped her phone somewhere into her sari, thanked Evelyn, and removed the baby from her arms. Evelyn posed for the next photo, moving through the crowd with grace, smiling, talking, being her curious mix of enchanting-humble, looking absolutely nothing like someone falling up stairs.

I wasn't sure about myself.

I wasn't sure about India.

I wasn't sure about love, relationships, and my fit for them.

I wasn't sure why she was so unsure about herself.

But I was sure about her: she had something.

13

## MANISH AND SONIA

Sitting in the hotel lobby, waiting for the opening party to start, I wrestled a ferocious digital opponent intent on choking my will—my will to check my spam e-mail. It looked good for a while. I pinned Indian Internet against the ropes. He fought back, though, busting out a devastating combo of his three signature moves: Buffer, Freeze, and BIG DADDY DISCONNECT.

KO'd, I put my phone in my pocket swearing to get my vengeance as Manish plonked down on the couch opposite. "I never thanked you," I said. "For your help in that field."

"Sounds like we were in a war together."

"We sort of were."

"Did we win?

"There were a lot of casualties. In my nerves."

"Well." He stuck out his tongue. "No need, buddy."

"No, really. Did you get back here okay?"

"Mate." His blinking slowed. "It was a disaster. My girlfriend just passed her driver's test, and to say it shows is like saying the Blue Man Group shows."

This was an improvement on the wriggling snake, but not by much.

"She's Indian too, right?"

"Last I checked. We're the only two Indians racing."

"Why would an Indian do this? Organised, I mean."

"Because all Indians own a rickshaw?"

"Feels that way."

"Well, I just moved back here."

His girlfriend, Sonia, arrived and fell like a falling piano into the seat next to him. Her unkempt thicket of shoulder-length hair gave Evelyn's a run for its money. Only hers was as dark as a joke where everybody dies at the end. Black she did well; it was the colour of her nail polish, her three nose rings, and her faded Metallica T-shirt. She was a long way from the groups of demure women we'd seen that day, so brightly coloured in wrapped fabrics they looked like flashmob rainbows. She reached across him for the cigarette packet on the glass coffee table. "I swear to God, Manish, if you've smoked all our cigarettes..."

"When did you get your licence?" I asked.

"A month ago." She took out a cigarette and rolled it between her fingers. "I must travel a lot for a new job so decided it was time. And what better way to practice than in a rickshaw, right?"

"How you finding it so far?"

"It'd be going better if you didn't try to kill us every five minutes, love," Manish said. He received a playful slap. "*Ow.* Come on. You've many good qualities, but your driving isn't one."

"That's why we're here!"

"It's why we won't be here long, yeah."

They were an enjoyable combo. "Where do you two live?"

"I'm in Bangalore. He's in Mumbai. *For now.*" It sounded like a threat.

I looked around for Evelyn. She must be still getting ready for the party. "Where did you two meet?"

They swapped sharp, suspicious looks. "If I tell you," Sonia said, "do you promise you won't tell anyone?"

"Who would I tell? I live far away."

"And you won't think all Indians get arranged marriages and it's still, like, feudal times over here?"

"I... err... promise, I guess?" I said, trying to imply how little my promises were worth. She kicked off her sandals, swivelled sideways, pushing her back against the sofa's edge, and stretched her legs across Manish's lap. "You know how dating works here, right? Parents talk to cousins who talk to friends who call their cousins. So many cousins. There's also a kind of Indian-dating Facebook. Anyway, eventually they find someone suitable and arrange dates."

Manish's expression flicked between a bright smile and a dim cringe.

"It's really awkward," she said. There was that word again. "You sit together and eat biscuits and drink tea while making fleeting eye contact. I told my parents no, that won't work for me. I'm a modern Indian woman. I don't need a man. I don't need to get married. I don't even like tea."

"Who doesn't like tea?"

"I like whisky. And driving."

"It doesn't like you," said Manish.

She raised her middle finger then slowly rotated it. "And I like sex. And Metallica. And cigarettes. So... *if* I marry. *If*! I'll marry who *I* choose, and I'll marry for love. Or lust, at the very least."

Evelyn wasn't the only open book around.

"My parents are quite modern. And so they said okay."

"That's what they all say, of course," said Manish. "You never know what they're scheming in the background. Mate, Indians are the world's best plotters."

"And so it was late one night," she said. "My mother called." She thickened her accent. 'Sonia. Now, Sonia. I know what I said. But this boy...'

"'Mum, stop.'

"'Sonia! He grew up in the UK. He's perfect for you.'

"'Stop.'

"'Just one phone call. That's it. Just one.'"

Manish laughed, his cheeks flapping like washing on a line.

"Indian parents, they're..." She searched for the right word. "Masters of soft power. So, anyway, we did the call, didn't we, darling, hunny bunny, schnookums." Her tone grew more bitingly sarcastic with each pet name. Then she reached over and pinched his cheeks. "I don't know. With him it was..." She took his hand. "Different." She squeezed it until he yelped in pain.

"That's it?" I said. "That's... nice. Why didn't you want to tell me that?"

"It's embarrassing."

"Why?"

"Because we don't need to date like that anymore. India's changed. People come to the megacities, places like Bangalore, where I'm from, and they just see the chaos and smog and corruption. People living in slums next to brand-new-already-falling-down mansions. What they don't understand is that the city, for a modern Indian, is freedom. Because there we're anonymous. Have you been to Bangalore?"

I nodded. I'd spent a week there on my last trip. It was a remarkable place—a small, unimportant provincial town that went to sleep one night only to wake up conquered by the armies of the future. A war it had lost before it even knew it was fighting. Now, it was a shiny, modern glass city of Indian migrants doing the white-collar jobs other countries had tired of. It scared me to imagine how big it had to be by now.

"No one is from Bangalore," she said. "We're all immigrants. We talk English to each other because it's the only common language we have. In the city, caste doesn't matter. Family is far away. We're free."

She and Manish exchanged a smile. No matter how hard they tried to hide their tenderness, it was there, bubbling just under the surface of their interactions. "And you and your girlfriend?" she asked.

*Girlfriend.* I didn't correct her. Love was in the air, and I had no desire for it to dissipate. "Evelyn. We met in a bar."

For the first time, I realised that if things went to plan—my plan—one day Evelyn and I would sit as comfortably as Manish and Sonia regaling people with the story of how we met, which would be the story of this stupid, terrifying race. I was sure we'd get very good at telling it. I was less sure anyone would believe it.

"Come on, mate," said Manish, before I'd even got to the race part. "Who still meets in a bar?"

## 14

## THE OPENING PARTY

His name was Lance. Of course his name was Lance. "Really stitched me up out there," he bellowed. It was like being in the front row of a Metallica concert. "Made me tip over!"

I took a step back. "Ah. That was you?" I knew it was him. He wasn't someone you missed in the same way football stadiums weren't something you missed. He didn't inhabit space—he conquered it, dominated it, made it cower, lip trembling, until he left.

"I stalled," I said. "Couldn't get out of the way."

"Uh-huh. Right." He ran a hand through thick ropes of his blond surfer's hair. Beneath them was a face chiselled from Mount Masculinity, its edges so sharp and pronounced you could have used them to open your beer.

"You all get out of the wreckage okay?" I asked.

"Few scars. But women like scars, aye?" he said, flexing his biceps, which already bulged under the sleeves of his fitted white shirt.

"I'll get you back," he said ominously.

The party was taking place in adjoining suites of the hotel's highest floor. Evelyn appeared beside me.

"How long have you two been dating then?" he asked.

"Oh, we're not," said Evelyn, making that love-cloud rain reality.

"Yeah. We're friends." I left a little weight on the word *friends*, a hint at an unexplored more.

"It's a funny story," she said. "We met in a bar the other night. My teammate broke her arm and I couldn't find anyone else at such short notice. Adam agreed the morning of the flight."

It was two days before, but I didn't correct her. The story was morphing. Was she making it more sensational? Or just forgetting it? So much for her impeccable memory.

"You just met? Geez." There was a certain something in the way he looked at Evelyn. At what he did with his tongue. He looked at her like he was... hungry. "Naaah, I'm not buying it. What about work?"

"This is work," I said. "I'm at work."

He scoffed. "Yeeeeah. No way."

He turned his supertanker frame towards his teammates—two fellow Aussies wider than they were tall, all thick hunks of prime-cut man meat. "Boyz, have a listen to this old crock."

Fifty-six of us were racing, most either British or German. We had an average age of thirty. "Highest ever," said Aarav, holding court at a table splattered with bottles, behind which two of the mechanics poured long drinks into highball glasses with a commendable disregard for accepted alcohol-to-soft-drink ratios.

"How did we do today?" I asked Pamir.

"One or two of you are good."

"The rest are terrible," said Aarav, sweeping his hand across the room. "Rubbish." He looked at me. "You're terrible."

I bristled. "Is this your day job? Running these races?"

"Yeah."

"Oh, I thought maybe you might be a motivational speaker?"

"Ha." He raised his glass in mock toast. "Bollocks to that!"

I tried to push the race from my mind. It belonged to tomorrow. Tonight, we would party. I'd get to meet the other racers and see Evelyn socialise, dance, and perhaps get drunk enough to realise I was the man of her dreams. I was unclear how much alcohol that might take but buoyed by the speed with which she was consuming it. Lance slid conspiratorially close to me. I tilted my head all the way back. Then across. Then back. Then across. I couldn't fit all of him into my view; it was like being in the front of an IMAX cinema. And the movie was *Rambo*.

"That Evelyn," he said. "Real beauty. You hitting that?"

I straightened. He still loomed thirty centimetres above me. "She's not a *that*."

"Come on, mate, you know what I mean." His *mates* were different from Manish's; more of a *maight*, as if our friendship were hypothetical when actually it was non-existent.

"I like her, yeah."

"But you're not doing anything about that?"

I shrugged. "I don't know. We just met."

"A woman like her." He whistled. "She needs to be shown who's in charge."

"Uh-huh."

"A woman like that wants an alpha. Yeeeah. She won't admit it, but that's what she wants."

"You know a lot about women, it seems?"

"I dabble." His team's name was Crouching Woman, Hidden Cucumber, which demonstrated all the nuance he showed the fairer sex. Evelyn was laughing now. Her eyes sparkled as she tipped Prosecco into her mouth. There was no way to let your eyes wander the room. They'd immediately home in on her and stick as firmly as we had on the vinyl seats of Toby's non-brother's non-restaurant.

"You know your problem, mate?" He tapped the side of his head. "You're overthinking it."

"How do you work that out?"

"None of it will matter in the end."

"It matters now, no?"

"No, mate. It really doesn't." He thudded off to get another drink, touching Evelyn on the elbow as he passed. I strained to listen to her conversation. "Do you like paying taxes?" a Canadian living in Bahrain asked her.

She considered it over another generous swig of her drink. "I've never really understood people's problem with taxes. I'd pay even more if I knew they'd use it right. Also, what's everyone's problem with the nanny state? I think, if anything, the state should have more nannies in it. I'd love a nanny or two popping in, or *Poppins in*? Ha. I'll stop."

The woman fell back onto her heels. "Guess the tax rate in Bahrain."

"Zero percent?"

"Oh." The woman frowned. "Yes."

I wandered over. Evelyn saw me, smiled, and linked her arm through mine. "Let's dance." I'd only just become a dancer. A private dancer. Part of a desire to think less and feel more. Lance wasn't exactly wrong in his analysis of me, which was extra annoying. I knew if I hesitated for even a second, I'd overthink things and become Evelyn on stairs. Arm in arm, we walked to the other suite, where a dozen people were already on the makeshift dance floor thrusting their hips, wiggling their behinds, and jerking their elbows to a bass-heavy Bollywood dance track. Evelyn glided in amongst them, rolling her shoulders, flicking her hair, a grin creeping its tendrils across her face. I tried to keep up, to stay focused on the music and not her, as the distance between us closed. She giggled, shut her eyes, raked a hand through her hair. She made the most of her curves yet was oblivious to their effect as she spun in a circle raising her arms up over her head.

One song slid into the next as the other people in the room faded from my attention. We took breaks to drink, to talk, to catch our breath.

Four days earlier I'd been in a bar celebrating how tightly I had circumstance by the neck. I was only in that particular bar because the first I'd tried had been full. Evelyn and I had fallen into conversation because the only free table was the one next to mine. We stayed talking because a few streets away, her friend was skipping a red light and crashing into the side of a taxi with enough force to knock Evelyn and me halfway across the world. It was dizzying to think of all the other timelines crowding this one, jostling and jumping and waving and begging us to swerve off and follow them through paths, possibilities, places, and people into moments very much *not* this moment. Life isn't what happens while you make other plans —it's what spites them.

I swirled her anticlockwise until my arm stretched, and then I flicked her back, spinning her towards me and taking her in my arms. Our faces moved together.

This was it.

This was the moment.

I leaned forward.

I pushed out my lips and closed my eyes.

Just six months ago I'd split from my previous girlfriend, Annett. I was still unsure how we'd lost control of the greatest friendship of my life. Loving someone is hard. Like a tuk-tuk race through India, it's full of hazards, forces you to face your fears, and can greatly shorten your life expectancy. It asks a lot of difficult questions, and I felt I'd fluffed many of the answers. Since the breakup, I'd carried the feeling of having failed a crucial test of my character. Shouldn't I take more time to study other people and fix myself before I went back into that examination room?

I opened my eyes and turned my head. The moment juddered past as the song ended. She dropped her hands from my waist. I stepped back to get a drink and Lance moved into my place.

The next time I looked he was grinding against her lower back. She turned. He bent down and forwards like a collapsing tree and kissed her.

I froze. Reality had gotten corrupted, somehow. I jerked, blinked, tried to fix it. Almost immediately Evelyn broke away and walked towards the exit.

Lance turned and slowly searched the room. I knew who he was looking for. As soon as he saw me, he winked. Why was everyone winking suddenly?

Oh, and also, HOW DARE HE!

*But, wait... why shouldn't he?*

It was stupid to think I'd be the only one to see it. And what claim did I have to her? She was out of my class, out of my league, out of my comfort zone. A distraction, a confusion, a source of poisonous Doubt, and a detour to a (admittedly very scenic) dead end.

I was here for India, the race, to overcome a fear, and to collect a bunch of great new stories and people. Evelyn was just the first; the catalyst. I could already add "Breakfast in France," Toby, Sonia, and Manish to the list. There would be many more to come.

An hour later, I found her in the other room with the mechanics. "Adam! There you are. This is Kumar, Rajesh, and Rohit." She gestured to them, the last of whom was Neutral-levergassee. "Lovely boys. We're having a lot of fun. I've been showing them the finer art of the perfect gin and tonic. Rohit is a natural. Although Kumar and Rajesh are none too shabby either." The boys served up a round of humble hewobbles, swooning in the heat of her attention.

She took my arm. "Dance with me!"

I shook my head. "I'd love to, but the tuk-tuk won't race itself tomorrow. I'm off to bed."

15

# RACE DAY ONE: TRIVANDRUM TO ALAPPUZHA

Some people would say four alarms is overkill. Killing was certainly on my mind when, at 6am, they combined in an unholy racket of blaring urgency that sent me leaping a full metre into the air. Evelyn scurried off to pacify them while I pulled a pillow over my head. Silence, when it finally came, had never sounded so sweet.

It's just a shame it lasted only a few minutes. And that I wasted it lying very still, very quietly, PANICKING WILDLY INSIDE, my head a cacophony of sirens all with one explicit aim: to make me run as fast as I could from the situation I was in.

Somehow, I ignored them. Because of her, I guess. And my ego. I didn't want to quit on either of them. And so, Evelyn and I shuffled down into the lobby, where we found four sheiks, three chauffeurs, two flower-power hippies, two samurais, Batman, Robin, and a giant, fluffy Chewbacca checking out and preparing their tuk-tuks.

"Did you know we were supposed to dress up, Evelyn?"

She looked up from composing the day's tenth e-mail on her overworked phone. It had been a long time since that thing had had a holiday. "I never quite got around to organising it."

"Morning all," croaked Manish, cuddling a silver thermos of coffee. He and Sonia were in full cricketers' whites. "When you putting your costumes on then?"

"No costumes," I said. "Why cricket?"

"Bloody love a bit of cricket."

"You too, Sonia?"

She'd accented her outfit with black lipstick. "This is very much him. I was... *busy*, mostly."

Lance strode over in a padded Superman suit. And there it was again—the jealousy, and with it, a lungful of wet, poisonous Doubt. *Does Evelyn like him? Does she go for men like him? Could I become a man like him?*

We had a staring contest that I lost quickly and emphatically. "Good aye, all," he growled.

"Hi," said Evelyn, her face betraying no emotion before she returned it to her phone.

"Sleep well? Excited?" he asked.

"Terrified," she said.

"You'll do—"

Aarav put two fingers in his mouth and let an ear-splitting whistle rip through the lobby. "Right, you horrible lot, outside."

We posed stiffly for a group photo and waited for another of his legendary pep talks. He rubbed his hands together, igniting the fire of his personality. "This, you silly, silly people, is *the* moment. THE MOMENT." He put all his teeth on window display. "Right, Pamir?"

Pamir's head sank forwards, ready for its date with the guillotine. He looked like I felt: certain, absolutely certain, that his long overdue demise had finally arrived. This was a terrible mistake, wasn't it? Why could only Pamir and I see this?

"You've had more than enough time to practice," Aarav

continued. He worked best alone anyway. "Now the carnage begins!" He picked up his air guitar and shredded an epic solo as the group whooped, hollered, and bounced off towards their tuk-tuks. "It's not too late," I said, as we dropped our bags into the backseat of ours. Evelyn nibbled on her lip. "It's too late. We'd never forgive ourselves."

And with those uplifting words, we climbed into our glorified shopping trolley and began the one-thousand-kilometre-long race. In the distance, an asthmatic grey mutt chuckled sinisterly.

It had only been twelve hours, but the tuk-tuk's controls felt foreign and unfamiliar in my hands: like a second language I'd not used since school and in which the only sentence I could remember was *big cow farts yoghurt fire*.

I inflated my lungs and blew out a long, slow breath, trying to mollify the stress and fear. It didn't work. I reached for the starter lever, pulled on it, and was rewarded with the engine's sultry, deep baritone. Sweat pooled at the base of my spine. Weather was a weapon here: a ray gun set to stun. But with no windscreen or doors, the tuk-tuk would at least provide whatever breeze the day offered.

I rolled us out of the parking space. At the car park's exit, Aarav swung an enormous green flag. The race had begun.

"Left or right?" I shouted. It was 6:30am, well before the commuter rush. The roads were quiet. Turning right would lead us upwards to a long overpass soaring into the distance like a concrete bird. Left, the road plunged down, towards a set of traffic lights.

"I don't know! The stupid phone's not working."

The junction got nearer. "Left or right?"

"It's... ugh..."

"LEFT OR RIGHT?"

"HMM. UGH. UHMM."

"Evelyn!"

I stayed left since it involved the least number of lane changes, and so we descended, passing a sign for the city centre. Wait, we needed to flee Trivandrum today, to strike out for the coast. Today belonged to edges, not centres. I looked up at the bypass and saw Lance's bulky frame spilling from the sides of the Australians' tuk-tuk pointing and laughing at me.

We'd gone the wrong way at the very first junction. We were going into the city. This was bad. Very bad. I hit the indicator, checked the mirror, and cut across to our right, hoping to make a U-turn and find my way back up onto the overpass. I made it across two lanes, but a bus blocked the final one, so I downshifted, slowing to let it pass, and then jumped onto the accelerator to zoom into the tiny gap it had left behind, forcing the tuk-tuk behind it to swerve to avoid me.

I was proud of this manoeuvre. It was a day-five manoeuvre, not an hour-one manoeuvre. I looked back. Evelyn's face was ablaze with white-hot fear.

"Are we still alive?" she said.

"I think so."

"It was touch-and-go for a while there though. I've already done about a football team's worth of Hail Marys."

"Marychester United?" The traffic lights were a bitter, uninviting red. The bus had made it through the junction in time, leaving me in my coveted far-right lane, at the front of a queue of sputtering exhausts. I turned to my left to thank the tuk-tuk driver who'd let me in. Not that he'd had a choice.

"Thanks!" I shouted.

"Hey! My tuk-tuk!"

"Sorry?"

"You hit me!"

"I hit you?"

"Yes."

He gestured at his back wheel. "You need to be careful."

I looked back but couldn't see any damage. If I'd hit him, it must have been more love tap than knock-out blow.

"I'm sorry," I said. "Can I do a U-turn here?"

He twisted in his seat and stared ahead. Evelyn leaned over. "Your being a good guy is noted and appreciated and will probably be rewarded someday, but the information pack says don't apologise. It's admitting you did something wrong."

"Oh," I said, and then followed it up with a sharp, "Hmm." This would be a tough rule for a Brit to follow. We never wait to sin before asking for absolution. "Did I clip his tuk-tuk?"

"I don't think so, no."

The light flashed a friendlier orange and I jumped on the throttle, beating every other vehicle through and buying myself a second to make the U-turn and nose in front of oncoming traffic. A policeman with a small orange baton shook his head.

It would take a lot more than that to stop me. I was here and I would not apologise.

Well, perhaps I would apologise. But that wasn't the point right now. The point was that I was here. Where I needed to be. Going the right way. Righting wrongs. Flashing my teeth and screaming into fear's face as, like a horny salmon, I slipped us upstream towards the overpass.

We were back on track.

16

## THE FIRST SHIFT

We slowly untangled ourselves from the city's sticky web. "HOW LONG HAVE I GOT LEFT?" I shouted back at Evelyn over the roar of the engine.

"THIRTY MINUTES."

How could I have been driving for only an hour? It felt ten times as long. And there were so many more hours like this one left. I opened the throttle of our piddly engine and tasted the heady rush of fourth gear, silently praying for the tuk-tuk to be nice to me, to humour all my fumbled gear changes as the road fell open before us, its edges dense with brilliant green vegetation.

A bus clattered behind us, almost close enough for its front windscreen wipers to be able to swish the dirt from our back window. I snarled at it in the rearview mirror as it swerved right to overtake us, pushing oncoming traffic left and us right—off the road and into the dirt. It edged past us then swerved violently in front of us as its driver spotted an upcoming bus stop. I jumped onto the brake. We jolted forwards in our seats.

"Mother... licker!" Evelyn shouted.

*Motherlicker?*

"I hate this. I hate them," I said, raining blows onto the horn after we'd come to a sudden, jerky stop. Boxed in, we waited for the bus's passengers to disembark. The driver budgeted three seconds, leaving passengers leaping to the curb like lemmings off a cliff. Then it pulled away, and like a cowed pet, I followed slowly behind it, tail between my legs.

I'd just made it into third gear when a scooter carrying two teenagers pulled level with us. The passenger spotted us and shouted into the ear of the driver, who pulled closer to our right-hand side. The passenger pulled out his phone and held it up, smiling into the camera, trying to get the four of us into one shot, leaning back, gripping the scooter with just his thighs.

The scooter strafed right. They were on the wrong side of the road and an approaching car hammered its horn in warning. As did the lorry behind it. They surged forwards regardless, the phone still aloft like a trophy they were presenting to a cheering crowd.

"Pull in," Evelyn shouted, waving them to the side. "We'll stop. You can take a photo."

*HONK HOOONNNNKKK*

The lorry was just a few metres away now. The scooter's driver hit the accelerator, darted in front of us, and then appeared on our left, where he slowed. His passenger swapped hands to try to get the photo with his left. It was like being pestered by a suicidal fly. Were they oblivious to the danger they were putting themselves in? Were we the only people who felt it—the overwhelming precariousness of everything?

It was an hour on the roads of India: sublimely awful and awfully sublime. We had five days and just short of a thousand kilometres left. "There's a fort coming up," Evelyn shouted. "Pull in there."

17

# ANCHUTHENGU FORT

Anchuthengu Fort did its job well. That job was to scream FEAR ME at its surroundings. We stood before its high, imposing stone walls scrutinising a tiny, innocent-looking black plaque with silver writing. On top of making our destination by sunset each day, we could also complete zany challenges for bonus points. Or so they'd said. To be honest, there's nothing particularly zany about finding a plaque and reading it to learn who had built a fort. The East India Company had built this fort, back in 1696.

"I don't know all that much about the British Raj," Evelyn said, as we walked along a red-brick pathway lined with flowering plants overwhelming their terracotta pots. There was a rare moment of shade as puffy, milky-white clouds billowed overhead.

"Not read an article on that then?"

"Sure. But it's not quite sticking, you know? How could so few people take over a whole country and hold it for so long?"

"I've been reading about it since we got here."

"They didn't teach you about it in school?"

"No. Not really."

"Why?"

"British history lessons are just an endless loop of the Second World War and how we saved the world and now everyone has to love us forever."

"Weird. Germans are obsessed with everything they've ever done wrong."

"Yeah, it's a national fetish."

She flogged her back. "Self-flagellation?"

"Exactly. And you did your most spectacular wrongdoing later, when everyone was watching. And, I have to say, with a real flair for the paperwork."

A picnicking Indian family smiled at us, beckoning us to eat with them. That was nice, but we didn't have time. We were in a race. Sort of. Against ourselves, mostly. At the entrance, I looked around for the tuk-tuk. "Where did we...? It was... err...?" I wasn't lost, of course. My mental map was merely recalibrating. Somehow nothing looked familiar. Evelyn watched on, grinning and tapping her foot.

"You done?"

"Erm."

She pointed over my shoulder. "The tuk-tuk's that way."

This was annoying, as I'd just at that very moment also decided that direction had to be where the tuk-tuk was parked. "I can keep driving if you like?" I said. "I think I've got the hang of it now."

"No."

"Sure? I don't mind." I minded.

"No."

"After an hour, you'll have it nailed."

She did a mock hewobble and slid into the front. I positioned myself at the side, my hand wrapped around the starter lever. Several race teams were parked in front of us, drinking milky chai from a roadside stall. I took off my baseball cap and tried to dam the stream of perspiration dripping into my eyes, then tugged the lever. The engine moaned. Evelyn slipped into first and overaccelerated. The tuk-tuk lurched forwards, crying out as if whipped. Everyone turned to see who was still so bad at driving their tuk-tuk. Evelyn was still this bad at driving her tuk-tuk. Although, in fairness, she'd only just started.

I got in. "Aaaarrgggh!" She shouted as we juddered out of the parking area. "Oh God. Oh no. Oh why. What are we? Stupid! Stupid! *Aaaahhhhh.* Okay. Fine."

She was progressing quickly through the stages of grief. "Oh wow," she shouted, ten minutes later, without turning her head, as she hit fourth gear for the first time and sped into acceptance. "This *is* so much nicer than driving in the city. Almost nothing is trying to crash into me. Except maybe that last lorry, and that car, and definitely that scooter there, and all those children," she said, as we passed a sign showing a dead body covered in a sheet: *SLOW DOWN! 77 FATALITIES IN THREE YEARS.*

They might as well have hung skulls.

# 18

# A SPECTACULAR TALE OF OLD-FASHIONED, NO-NONSENSE BARBARITY

The East India Company's takeover of India is a story of incredible audaciousness, greed, and old-fashioned, no-nonsense barbarity. A David and Goliath affair that begins in 1599, on the outskirts of London, England: a culturally and economically irrelevant nation contributing a whopping 3 percent to the world's GDP.

That is about to change.

That change will come because of a genius new idea, a kind of economic timeshare called a joint-stock company (a precursor to the public limited company): a clever bundle of contracts and legal fictions that allows anyone to buy and sell shares in a company's future profits. With it, even lowly paupers and urchins can become speculators, investors, and asset owners. The company founded on this day is the East India Company. The builders of Anchuthengu Fort.

They are our story's David.

David's investors dig deep within their breeches and pool enough money for the company to buy three pirate ships. One is called, and I kid you not, the *Scourge of Malice*. They rename it the *Red Dragon*, which is only slightly less terrifying. With these ships they plan to race the Dutch into the East Indies and establish a spice-trading route—an incalculably risky venture in a time where everyone is at war with everyone and there are more cut-throat pirates in the seas than dignified nobles on the lands.

David sets sail. It starts badly when, just off Dover, the wind cuts out and those threatening ships are left stranded for weeks. They're so close to the shore they can almost hear the laughter rippling through London's taverns and dock—laughter at the foolhardiness of their endeavour. Eventually the wind returns and blows them as far as the Strait of Malacca, where they meet a Portuguese ship bobbing low in the opposite direction, laden with spices. East India wants spices. Here are spices. They're someone else's spices, sure. But you can't have everything, right?

*Wrong*. You can have everything if you're not hampered by morals. In its first hostile takeover, the East India Company steals the spices and sails back home, where it sells them for a cool million pounds.

It's easy, this spice-trading lark, so David keeps sailing and robbing. He even makes it to the Indies, where he discovers it's way too late—the Dutch are already there and have better ships, deeper pockets, more collegial relationships, and Rembrandt.

They're really having a moment, the Dutch.

David needs a new plan. He scours around for something else he can trade. What do people need? He scratches his head. He stares forlornly into the middle distance. He rolls up his shirt sleeves.

Sleeves! That's it! "Eureka!" he shouts, possibly. "We'll trade textiles!"

But who is making the best textiles of the time, you ask? That would be the Mughal Empire: the richest, most advanced state on earth. It produces the finest art, architecture, weaving, music, and jewellery. It's responsible for a whopping 38 percent of the world's GDP and controlling most of what we now call India, Pakistan, Bangladesh, and Afghanistan.

They are this story's Goliath.

The East India Company's former pirate ships sail off towards this great, glittering jewel of an empire. An empire that barely notices their arrival. Slowly, quietly, David makes his first trades, and a few boats of cloth and silk float back towards Blighty. He makes a modest profit, which is reinvested in East India's first trading post, in Surat.

The year is 1619.

Orders increase and slowly David expands his operation, opening more trading posts and warehouses, which grow to become factories and entire ports around which cities like Calcutta and Bombay form. And all of it belongs to the East India Company. Those grubby pirates become legitimate businessmen.

Then something unforeseen happens—the mighty Mughal Empire falls. Its new emperor, Aurangzeb, is a stickler: a stickler for Islam. Many faiths have long coexisted peacefully under the Mughals but he changes this, running around like an angry child on a beach, knocking over other faith's sacred sites as if they're sandcastles. He restores a tax on the Hindu faith and goes on an expansionist rampage to the beaches of the south, where his appetite for conquest bites off more than his war machine can chew. The empire has peaked and his enemies know it. Slowly, his subjects turn on him. By the time he's replaced by a playboy named Muhammad Shah, the Mughal glory days are over. And on the other side of the mountains of the Khyber Pass, a ferocious Persian warrior and gifted military strategist called Nader Shah waits. Sensing the Mughals are weak, he marches his army over from Iran.

The year is 1739.

His army meets a Mughal cavalry of three hundred thousand men and two thousand war elephants. That's right: *war elephants*. He's outnumbered six to one. But Nader Shah has a secret weapon: swivel guns loaded on camels. That's right: *swivel camels*.

Tactics, technology, and ruthlessness end the Battle of Karnal after just a few hours. Emperor Shah is captured and accepts defeat. Six weeks later, Nader Shah, is the Mughal Empire's new ruler, is in Delhi collecting the spoils and leaving for Iran with a modest eight thousand waggons' worth of the empire's finest glittering swag. A loss that grinds the Mughal's economic engine to a juddering halt.

Where's David in all this? The East India Company is still on the coast, as before, trading away. Around the company's ports, the Mughal Empire implodes; each state wars with the next, but none are as trained or armed as the East India Company, which rocks the latest military thinking and hardware from Europe. East India strongholds are calm—there's rule, order, and working courts. You can lend and borrow money and trust in a legally enforceable tomorrow. David spreads out, borrowing, lending, securing, taking over more and more of what was Mughal business until he reaches Bengal: the Mughal finance centre. Here, David looks around and realises he has no serious, credible competition. Goliath, or what's left of him, has given up. So, just as he did with that Portuguese ship some hundred and fifty years earlier, he reaches out and grabs what he wants.

The East India Company grabs India. The year is 1757. A private company, run from a head office in London with fifty staff, owns an empire. Perhaps unsure how long they can hold it, they promptly begin asset stripping in a frenetic, unsustainable way. Hundreds of millions of dollars' worth of loot disappears on boats bound for England, where it lines the pockets of East India's shareholders, of which 25 percent of the British Parliament now call themselves.

Within five years, the damage is done. The Indian economy is decimated, its treasuries plundered. In 1771, a famine breaks out in Bengal that kills ten million people. David (now really a Goliath himself) does nothing to stop it. He answers only to his shareholders. All the while, so many ill-gotten gains are flooding through the docks of England that questions start being asked in Parliament. *Hasn't the East India Company got a little big for its boots? Isn't it now a de facto nation-state? Under whose authority does it operate? Why is it not obligated to help the starving masses of Bengal? Why does a private company need an army of 260,000, twice the size of the entire British army?*

These questions are answered unsatisfactorily, but David has finished picking the Mughal Empire's bones clean anyway. The company returns home and declares itself bankrupt.

The year is 1858.

East India then pioneers the too-big-to-fail ploy, since 40 percent of the British government is comprised of East India shareholders. A bailout is agreed, after which they hand India over to the British government to run. But by now India is so hobbled it's contributing just 7 percent to the world's GDP. Which is where it finds itself today, still recovering from this period in its history, slowly rebuilding its once glittering empire and working out what to do with places like Anchuthengu Fort.


Note: This chapter owed a large debt to two books—*The Anarchy* by William Dalrymple and *Inglorious Empire* by Shashi Tharoor. If you want a more comprehensive review of The East India Company and The British Raj, they're the place to look.

19

## THE FIRST BREAKDOWN

Sitting in traffic, I spotted a learner-driver up ahead and pointed. From the backseat, Evelyn let out a loud, shoulder-shaking laugh. "What do you think the lessons are like?" she asked. It was my shift again. I slid back in my seat to better hear as she mimicked an Indian accent. "This is the accelerator, this is the brake. You won't need the brake."

"You sound like Aarav."

"Oh. *That guy*."

As if to prove our point, a family of five squeezed past us on a single scooter: father in front, mother in back, surfing the exhaust, and three kids squashed between them like human jam.

Helmets worn? *None*.

"Are we nearly there yet?" I said, like a five-year-old on his way to Disneyland.

"No," she replied gruffly. How long since I'd last asked? Five minutes? Ten? Ooze dripped from deep wounds on my hands as I let out another deep, rasping, throat-shredding cough. Being in the open air meant we had a breeze but were inhaling everything carried in on it.

We were on Route 66, approaching Alappuzha, our destination for the night, idling in traffic beside a fruit stall whose owner slept with his head against the edge of his cart. It was easy to find romance in these roadside dreamscapes. To mistake poverty for innocence and confuse people who had little with those who wanted it. The traffic cleared, and we zipped over a white bridge—the latest freshly painted link across an unbroken chain of lagoons, lakes, and rivers. Canal boats packed with spices cut lines in the tranquil water, scattering clouds of white egrets into the sky. Kerala is spice country: its fertile wetlands grow what its narrow canals transport. The Venice of India, they call it. It was easy to see why.

The scenery was spectacular, my mood less so. The traffic cleared and after the next speed bump, I twisted the gearshift towards me only for it to lock in my hands.

"It's stuck," I said, as the engine pleaded for second gear.

"STICK?"

"STUCK. NOT WORKING."

"WHO'S TWERKING?"

"I'M PULLING IN." I said, stopping just past two roadside restaurants.

A breakdown on day one? How temperamental were tuk-tuks? I pulled out my phone: 5pm. Only a few hours until dusk. The day's points were in jeopardy.

"What happened?" Evelyn said, coming around to the front.

"It's stuck in first. Let's give it a break."

A kind-hearted pedestrian arrived immediately. "Problem?" he asked.

"It's stuck in first."

He hewobbled in agreement, neither surprised nor concerned. A second man appeared behind him. A third then manifested from under the second's hat, who pulled a fourth from his sleeve. The group then doubled themselves using concealed mirrors until—hey presto—they'd become a crowd. A helpful crowd who surrounded the vehicle and discussed, collectively, how best to solve the clutch problem. Evelyn and I looked on from two tiny, wobbly stools at a nearby fruit stand.

"You must love this?" Evelyn said.

"Why? I don't like this kind of attention."

"You don't look very uncomfortable. And you *need* this, no?"

There was a thread here, but I couldn't tug it loose. "Why would I *need* it?"

"For your book."

"I'm not writing a book."

"Nonsense. Why else would you be here?"

She was the biggest part of why I was here. I'd not mentioned what happened with Lance. Not that much had happened with Lance. Nothing she'd started, or seemed to want. And I was busy forgetting anything had happened with Lance. And that Lance existed. Which would have been easier if he weren't so enormous and loud and shameless and muscular. He did to rooms what the East India did to empires.

"I'm not." I paused. "I mean, maybe. You never know how things will develop. Sometimes what you think will be a great story just isn't, while a simple trip to the shop for yoghurt escalates and you lock yourself out, fall into a puddle, spend the last of your money on magic beans, and end up duelling a giant in the clouds. It seems like you can't really influence it."

"Oh, come on, as soon as something goes wrong you whip out your notepad."

"That's just habit," I said, looking down at the notepad on my knee, which I'd just put there, out of habit. "If you don't know what you need, you need everything."

"You need stuff to go wrong."

"All fixed," said the group's lead magician.

"Wow. Really?" It had taken the hive-mind less than five

minutes. This country did both hospitality and roadside-breakdown service right.

Evelyn turned to me, her eyes narrowing. "Was there really something wrong with the gearshift?"

"Of course," I protested. "Come on. Seriously?"

"It's just weird that it's fixed in like a minute, no?" Her tone wasn't angry, more mischievous, as if I had a secret I wouldn't let her in on.

"You think I'd fake a breakdown?!"

"Good story, no?"

I stood up and brushed the dust from my behind. "Do you think, maybe, that you might have some trust issues?" I said, as I began the extensive thanking, handshaking, and gratitude-displaying that my culture mandated.

And then we were back on the road. Another hour ticked by in the firm grip of intense, exhausting concentration. With thirty minutes before flag-down, all our mobile Internet used up, leaking blood and pus from a mosaic of hand wounds, we bumped into Sonia and Manish and followed them the last few kilometres to the hotel, where Aarav was waiting, waving a chequered flag.

I never thought I'd be so happy to see him. Or so happy full stop. "We did it!" Evelyn shouted, tooting the horn. I sat back, closed my eyes, and savoured the moment. When I did finally step down to the asphalt, I was so light with relief it was like walking on the moon. I went to high five Evelyn, but she knocked my hand aside and wrapped me in a hug worthy of day five, not day one.

"Oh, my God, I can't believe it's actually over," she said, beginning some parking-space yoga. "I don't know if I've ever been this tired. I feel like I used up a year's worth of adrenaline today. Even when you're in the back, you're not relaxed, you know? Because you're still helping and navigating and looking for suicidal cows. But we did it. Even though we're scared and we suck. We did it."

"One down, four to go." We'd had a sixty-minute break for lunch, thirty minutes at the fort, and fifteen during the one-hundred-percent-genuine breakdown—ten hours of driving to cover just one hundred and fifty kilometres. And even after all that slogging, we'd still arrived in nineteenth place. Tomorrow we had eighty-five kilometres further to cover than today.

We would have to get up very, very early, drive much more recklessly, or invent teleportation.

## 20

# RACE DAY TWO: ALAPPUZHA TO CALICUT

The hotel car park, 6am. I'd never known exhaustion like it. I felt as if I were carrying my own body weight in potatoes on my back. "Somehow," said Aarav, "and we had big bets against you, you all made it yesterday." It was hard to tell whom I disliked more: Aarav or Lance. "So, in our desperate search for hilarious entertainment, we're making things trickier today. Upping the ante. Aren't we, Pamir?"

Aarav's giant, reclusive henchman was always at his shoulder, staring forlornly into the distance. He was a man who was sure that not only had it already happened, but it was about to happen again. A man who always thought he could smell fire. A man whose silver linings turned out to be lead. He crossed his arms as Aarav flashed his trademark loathsome grin.

"Couldn't have said it better myself, Pamir. So today is even longer. Two hundred and thirty-five kilometres! And many truly awful roads."

"Awful," Pamir confirmed.

"Yep. We've hand-selected the most shit-kicking, ass-bruising, coccyx-busting, flea-bitten, hellhole roads this land has to offer. I wouldn't drive them for all the money in the world. But you will. *Today*. In a bloody rickshaw. So off you go then."

"Two hundred and thirty-five kilometres," Evelyn said with a whistle, as we walked towards the rickshaw eating our breakfast biscuits. The only breakfast we had time for. "How the hell are we going to do that?"

"It's a fine question."

"Yeah, but do you have an answer?"

"Skip lunch?"

"Yay. This trip is proving to be a fantastic diet."

We reached the tuk-tuk, and Evelyn patted its roof.

"How did we do yesterday?" I asked. "As a team, I mean. I got snappy when you didn't know the next direction sometimes."

"That's okay. You're under pressure and the phone's slow and the maps are useless and *blah*."

"You can get angry at me back, though. You can scream, shout, throw things. Call me a mother, what was it, *licker*?"

"Why would I do that?"

"Because I probably will. Not lick my mother, I mean. Well, there was this one time. But I will get snappy and shout at you. And it would be nice to not be the only unreasonable one on this team."

"But it would be..."

"Awkward?"

"Unnecessary," she said. "I thought you did really well with the driving. You got us out of that wrong turn. I couldn't have done that."

"Why didn't you say that then?"

"Erm. I just did?"

"Yeah, because I'm pushing you to."

She tutted. "I'm just not used to this."

"This what?"

"Talking about feelings, I think."

"You didn't do that with your boyfriends?"

She had a lot of stories about dates but far fewer about relationships. Which I guess are just dates that don't end.

"I didn't have those kinds of boyfriends."

"What kind did you have?

"The bad kind."

"What's your longest relationship?" I asked, expecting another dodge.

"Eight months."

Laughter slipped out before I could contain it.

"Don't laugh. I work a lot. And I have terrible taste, it seems."

The tuk-tuk was loaded and ready to go. "Who do you pick?" I asked, fumbling in my pockets for the keys.

"Men who chase me. I used to think that would mean they really wanted me, but I know there's a flaw in that logic. Those men are into challenges. Once they have you, well, there's no challenge."

My instincts had been right: I shouldn't chase her. But then how do you catch what doesn't want to be caught? Or get caught by what doesn't own a net? Not that I was chasing her. I was here for India, remember?

"I don't even blame them," she said.

"Why not?" I blamed them. How dare they have the audacity to get the woman I wanted but then not even want her?

"I don't know. Is it fair to ask someone to love you if you don't love yourself?" She stepped towards the driver's seat. "Let's get this tuk-tuk on the road. I'll start."

## 21

## RABBITS

"What's the bonus challenge for today?" she asked. We were halfway through my first shift, out of Alappuzha, cruising more of Kerala's backwaters. It was a long way to Calicut.

"Selfie with cow," I lobbed back over my shoulder.

"Pull into a back road?"

We were soon bouncing down a dusty alley passing yards with wire fencing, behind which mangy chickens pecked at the dirt. There'd be a cow around here somewhere. We'd seen many of these four-legged, vacant-eyed VIPs stumbling around like town criers, ringing the bell around their necks, announcing the news of their own arrival, silently cursing humans under their hot breath for what they'd bred them to become. Why India is so enamoured with them is open to debate. The most popular theory says that it's because Hindu scriptures venerate them. They've even awarded them their own goddess: Kamadhenu. But then Hinduism has a the-more-the-merrier approach to deities. Another theory says cows are hallowed because they're our ersatz mother; their milk nourishes us once our matriarch's stops.

"Did you...?" Evelyn poked me in the shoulder with an

empty water bottle. The slower speed made it easier to talk. "Unbelievable!"

"I have high water needs!" I protested. We were now sharing water bottles—another new intimacy marker reached. One that meant Evelyn wasn't getting much water. I remembered a documentary I'd once seen that explored why men are taller than women, as such a large height disparity isn't common in the animal kingdom. Perhaps it was because men hunted while women gathered? Or that women favoured tall men, which gave them a reproductive advantage that slowly stretched men like cooked spaghetti?

The documentarians made a thorough investigation. And they concluded no to both.

While no one could be sure, they found it just as likely that, for tens of thousands of years, men had hogged the calories for themselves. If karma were real, there'd be only women left, tall as basketball players, procreating asexually like starfish.

Up ahead, a gate opened and two boys emerged from it. Of all the things they'd expected to greet them, we—a novelty blue tuk-tuk with a historically starved and now also dehydrated blonde woman, along with her large pan-ethnic suitor—were likely low on the list. They toppled backwards into each other and then jumped up and down, waving their tiny arms until we stopped.

"Hello," I said. "Do you know where we can find a cow?"

Their eyes widened.

"C-O-W. MOO."

They turned to each other. No words came, so I emitted another loud "MOOOOOO" and upped the ante with a sideward head swivel below index finger horns. It was a frightfully good impression. Any better and I'd have been so confused I'd have milked myself. Yet, understanding eluded them.

They were obviously brothers, different chapters in the same book of biology. The smaller had rosy cheeks and a mischievous glint in his oval brown eyes. The older hid under a pudding-bowl haircut and held a purple cardboard box on his outstretched forearms. The younger opened its lid.

"*R#'#+ß!*" he said. I looked at Evelyn, who shrugged. From our seated positions, we couldn't see inside the box.

"*Ra*#+ß!*" Little Brother repeated.

"Rubbish?" Evelyn guessed. "I think he's asking if we have any rubbish?"

"Oh, that's nice," I said, scratching around the tuk-tuk to gather up the detritus of a "you should know better" diet: chocolate wrappers, crisp packets, and bottles of liquid I'd drunk more than my share of. I passed them to Evelyn, and she leaned out of the tuk-tuk and dropped them into the box.

"No!" the boy shouted, his saucer-wide eyes silently screaming at the injustices of the world. "Ra**#+t."

"Ah! Rabbit!" said Evelyn, tipping back into her seat. All the blood in her body gushed into her face. "We just literally trashed his rabbit!"

"Rabbit!" the boys repeated excitedly. "Rabbit!"

Everyone understood, except perhaps the rabbit. Big Brother lowered the box so we could get a good look at the mangy creature the colour of burnt toast, now wearing my Cheetos packet as a hat. "Cute!" said Evelyn, stroking it while removing the wrapper with excellent sleight of hand. The boy looked on proudly.

"Will you eat it?" I asked, pointing at the rabbit and then at their mouths while making a chewing gesture.

"NO! No!" Big Brother said, slamming the box shut then turning and darting for the gate so quickly that he kicked up a cloud of dirt. Little Brother ran along after him and then the gate thudded shut behind them. I collapsed in the driver's seat, gripping my stomach, laughing until all air abandoned me and tears danced down my face. Evelyn groaned in the back, cradling her head in her hands. "It's not *funny*."

"It so is."

"We just insulted them!" She pointed at the gate. "*Twice.*"

"Yeah, but we didn't mean to."

"So?" Her face was the colour of tomato soup. "That doesn't matter."

"It'll give them a good story."

"Not everything is about good stories." She sighed. "Another one for the worst-of-Evelyn reel, I guess."

I sat up. "You have a worst-of reel?"

"You don't?"

I tried to think of anything embarrassing I'd ever done... Nope, there was nothing. The slate of my memory was as smooth as marble. "How often is yours playing?"

"All the time, in the background. Isn't it for everyone?"

"Nope," I said cheerily. "I don't save the bad stuff."

She considered this, her nose twitching, not unlike a rabbit. "You actually like yourself, don't you? It's not an act? In the beginning, I thought it had to be. But... you're calm differently from most people."

"I mean, there've been some phases. And I have my weak points. But yeah, I find myself to be okay enough." I declined to mention my Achilles heel, or perhaps my Achilles high heel: women. There, I was timid, and regularly drowning in poisonous Doubt.

She ruminated on this. "It's a superpower."

"I found it odd at morning break when you asked if I thought the other racers liked us."

"That's a normal thing to worry about in a new group."

"I just noticed it had never crossed my mind. I mean, I care what you think about me. And my friends. But strangers, casual acquaintances, Australians?" I waited for her to bristle. She didn't. "You really don't like yourself? You're extremely likeable. You disarm people easily. Five minutes after you meet them, they're already telling you their life story."

I knew how easily it happened because it had happened to me. After just two hours of conversation I'd agreed to follow her halfway around the world. "It depends," she said, ducking my compliment as usual. "How I feel about myself changes a lot each day."

My mind fizzed and sparked. A new connection was wired: this was why social situations stressed her out—stressed all socially anxious people out. She entered each one willing to update her sense of self based on how the people in the interaction reacted to her. This was why what had just happened with the rabbit mattered. When she failed socially, she lost a little of whatever self-esteem she'd collected up. Awkwardness was a general, unspecific sense that a social interaction was going wrong, was about to slip off the tracks of etiquette and crash directly into her idea of herself.

I thought back to the fortress of the self. That fortress has a bouncer: ego. Ego stands at its door and decides what's allowed in. I didn't worry too much about what happened in the world, or what I exposed myself to, because my ego was at the door keeping negativity out, allowing me to keep seeing myself how I wanted to be seen. It wasn't like this for people like Evelyn. Ego wasn't on her side. Didn't protect her. Left the door to her fortress swinging open in the breeze.

Perhaps that was even why people with low self-esteem put themselves down. They decided it would hurt less to rob themselves than to be robbed by others. They broadcast that their fortress was empty of anything of value, so that no one would bother to break in. And it probably worked, but it came with a high cost.

If you tell people you have nothing of value to offer often enough, they'll believe you. If someone tells you they suck, who are you to tell them they're wrong?

She was wrong, and full of riches. Everyone else could see it even if she couldn't. I just needed to show her somehow.

## 22

## CHAI BREAK

*When will this day end? Will it ever end? Why does it have so much driving in it?* I took a gulp of the day's second roadside chai. We'd budgeted five minutes for it, and I intended to savour them all.

"What do you think *that* is?" Evelyn pointed at a coil of golden-brown pastry.

I signalled the seller. "I'll put it in my mouth and let you know."

"That's so unfair. How are you so skinny?"

"I'm not skinny."

"Do you know why skinny people are considered attractive?"

*Is she saying she considers me attractive? Is she saying she wouldn't if I ate too many more of these mysterious golden coils?*

"Sure." I lunged for an answer I was sure must be on a shelf in my mind. "Oh. Wait," I said, finding nothing. I'd just considered it self-evident that thinness was attractive.

"Well, I read an article about it once," she said. "I don't know if it's true, but it's interesting. It said that in the West, we see slim people as the physical ideal because they represent self-restraint in a world of abundance. That if they're not at home spooning tubs of Ben & Jerry's, they can probably resist spooning the neighbour."

"Fascinating." As well as light, she radiated interestingness.

"How long to go?" she asked.

"It's..." I realised—totally out of character for me—that I'd forgotten both where we'd come from and where we were going. I knew exactly where we were: we were by the side of a road. What road? Who knew. Someone, presumably, but not me.

Her phone rang. It would be a journalist looking for a quote from one of her politicians. I could often hear her tapping away when she wasn't driving. As we gain knowledge about our partners, we discover things about them that are annoying but also—for better or worse until annoyance do us part—part of their package. I suspected Evelyn was addicted to her work. Her work mattered, and I respected her dedication to it, but it didn't seem to give her all that much respect in return.

My package had a major flaw too: I'd want to write about her. To honestly, unflatteringly, throw whole conversations of ours over the fence into the public's yard. That was a lot to ask of someone. Especially someone who would wait to see what the public thought of her before deciding what *she* thought about her.

As Evelyn talked into her phone, nonchalantly holding a conversation with people on a different continent, a tuk-tuk blew its horn and indicated the wrong way, forcing a lorry to slam on its brakes and veer off through a parking space. The tuk-tuk bounced to a stop with the help of a low mud wall. Heavy metal music blared from its speakers. Its driver's seat was a tangled mesh of spindly black hair.

Only one person drove that badly: *Sonia*. Manish rolled

out the back of the tuk-tuk and collapsed into the dirt, clutching his stomach in laughter. "Did... you... see... *that*?"

"How could we miss it?" said Evelyn, ending her call.

"Great stuff, love," Manish said, getting up and wrapping her in a one-armed hug. "Your best parking attempt yet."

"How you two getting on?" Evelyn asked.

"We're doing much better today. You only nearly killed us, what, ten times, love?"

"If you criticise my driving again, I *will* kill you. But it will be with my hands and a smile on my damn face."

They stood with us as the traffic roared past. "We thought we saw you earlier," Sonia said. "But it's difficult to stay together in this traffic." We'd see another race team every hour or two, but driving in convoy was more trouble than it was worth. "How long's left?" Sonia asked.

Evelyn checked the map on her phone. "At least three more hours."

Sonia put a finger-gun to her temple and pulled the trigger. "This was a mistake, wasn't it?"

We nodded, falling into silence, staring at the ground. "When did you move back to India?" I asked Manish, hoping for a distraction.

"About three months ago."

"Do you miss England?"

"Does a desert miss shade?"

"*Erm?*"

"I miss cheddar. I miss sarcasm. I miss the BBC. I even miss chavs. I miss..." He hesitated. "It will sound kind of stupid, but I miss the mental calm that comes from knowing the thing you're about to do, while it won't be easy, will have a process that's well defined."

"I know what you mean," I said. "When you're young, you think rules are bad. Once you get older, you see their upside."

"There's a middle ground for sure. Too many rules and you're playing cricket."

"But you love cricket?"

"Not everything you love loves you back."

I thought about Evelyn and her job. "But you've Sonia here, at least."

"Yeah, but you've seen her drive. I won't have her for long."

*Whack*. An arm was punched. I need not say whose. I was getting a feeling for Sonia and Manish's package—she had to accept merciless teasing while he had to tolerate small acts of violence whenever large acts of language failed her.

It sounded like a fair trade to me.

## 23

## SO, WHERE DID YOU TWO MEET?

The lights of the garden restaurant hung in loose loops between the spikes of palm-tree leaves. A waiter emerged from the kitchen holding a plate heaped with food.

"Who had the...?" He looked down at the dish. "It's..." Four waiters with nests of plates and bowls crashed into his back, creating a multiarmed, multimealed dinner Krishna.

"Shrimp curry?" he shouted hopefully into the night. Fifty people arriving for dinner at once would overwhelm most kitchens. Ordering in India is a culinary hook-a-duck: everyone gets a prize but no one knows what. If they served us at least one thing we'd ordered, we considered that a success. With everything this delicious, what did it matter?

"SHRIMP CURRY! SHRIMP CURRY!"

Somehow, five minutes after sunset, we had trundled dazed, confused, and full of regret over the finish line. Twelve hours of driving! *Twelve.*

I poked at the skewers lying before me.

"What did you order?" Evelyn asked, hovering at my shoulder.

"I don't remember," I said, nibbling at the stick. *Coconut... Cinnamon... Lamb?*

"SHRIMP CURRY! SHRIMP CURRY!"

I looked across the table at my conversation partner, Robert. He was Dutch, in his early forties, and had a narrow face with a precise, cartoon-mouse nose. He was racing with his wife, Kirsty, and they were unusual for the group: older, quieter, didn't pride themselves on how much they could drink.

"Are you enjoying the race?" he asked. "I could imagine so, getting to spend time with your girlfriend, or perhaps because of the high expectations, it is less good than you expected, maybe, or even better? Better, yes?"

I put the skewer down. This was a spectacular question. I wanted to bask in the rays of its glorious inspecificity. Evelyn was in conversation with her neighbour, so I let the girlfriend thing slide, enjoying the jolt of pride that it gave me.

"The race is really intense. And being together so much it's... *intense*." I'd said *intense* twice. I was bungling this.

"And how are you finding India? As you expected or perhaps different from the last time you travelled here? Which you did. Some years ago. No?"

Since meeting Evelyn, I'd been thinking a lot about conversation styles. Small Talk is easy because there are topic templates you can follow—the weather, sport, what you did that day, children and how they say the funniest things. It's benign by design. Large Talk—the exchange of the meaningful between minds not tuned to each other's frequencies—is troublesome. We've all developed our own strategies to maximise the frequencies on which we broadcast, to increase the chance someone will hear our signal. Robert knew asking questions was good: that they were a proxy for interest. But questions only work if they feel personal. There's no point asking someone with vertigo about their latest bungee jump. So he tried to include proof that he could, if pushed, already guess how I would answer his questions. Only he didn't know, so he had to include all possible answers in his monster, run-on lines of enquiry.

"SHRIMP CURRY! SHRIMP CURRY!"

"What do you do for work?" I asked. *Generic. Lazy.* But it had been a long day with far too much *me* in it.

"Outsourcing," he said. "You know about outsourcing, yes? Or perhaps not? I think yes? I run a private newsletter where, each quarter, we interview the five big outsourcing companies about developments in outsourcing."

"Who reads it?"

"The five big companies, mostly."

"Does outsourcing change that much in a quarter?"

"No."

"Are you interested in outsourcing?"

"Yes." His eyes betrayed him. "Not really, no."

Two tables over, a shout of "Aussie, Aussie, Aussie!" rang out. "Oi, oi, oi!" A drinking contest was taking place and tables and backs were being slapped. I knew how each night would end for team Crouching Woman, Hidden Cucumber: with the world swirling like water down a drain. Lance had been over earlier fussing over Evelyn, faking an interest in her day, trying to get her to join their table. Asking her to settle a bet about who of the three of them was the most handsome. They were, somehow, all the most handsome.

"Aussie!"

"Oi!"

"Aussie!"

"Oi!"

"And how about you?" I asked Kirsty.

"I help him with the newsletter."

"Is it nice to work together?"

"Yes."

They were physical opposites: she had cropped spiky hair and a wide, unforgiving face that held the magnificent beaming eyes of a quizzical owl. Her movements were similarly slow and pronounced; almost animatronic. She sat, her head angled, blinking powerfully. Had the restaurant been quieter, I was sure I'd be able to hear whirring and clicking sounds.

"I'm not sure I could imagine working with my partner," I said.

"UHHM."

"I mean, it must have its upsides?"

"UHHM," she said, with another deafening, clunky blink. What was her conversation strategy and why wasn't it working on me?

"You get to spend a lot of time together, I guess? I'm just not sure I should subject someone to myself for too much of each day."

"UHHM."

"And definitely not in the morning. I'm awful in the morning. My friend Nick says I've got one good hour in me per day. After that my personality goes flat like coke that's lost its lid."

"UHHM."

The *uhhm*. That was it. We all need reassurance the other person in the conversation is enjoying us. But her *uhhm* sounded like a parody of people's interested sounds. I felt like a stand-up comedian in front of an audience that wasn't laughing. The temptation to turn on my own material increasing. It was lonely in the conversation with her. "Anyway, I'm wittering on."

"Where did you two meet? At work, perhaps?" Robert asked. We were getting this question a lot. It must have been an approved Small-Talk question for couples. Or suspected couples.

Evelyn was talking to Simon, a Malaysian man now living

in Dubai. "I've the best story for that," Simon interrupted, tearing greasy strips off a tennis-racket-sized piece of garlic naan. "It's how my grandparents met."

The owl swung her gaze to him. "UHHM."

"So, my granddad is Japanese and my grandmother is Malay. My granddad came over on the boat to Malaysia. Everyone in South East Asia hates the Japanese, as you probably know? They colonised most of the region at some point and were *very* brutal about it. So my granddad arrives and is treated badly by the locals. He's an outsider. A fisherman. Dirt poor. Then one day he sees my gran. She works at the market selling vegetables. Stirs something within him, I suppose. But he can't speak Malay and so can't communicate with her. He just watches her. Goes to the market and just sits, watching."

The curtain in my mind opened, revealing a stage with these two characters on it, under brilliant lights. You could almost smell the fish. See how this lowly, hardworking fisherman gazed forlornly at the innocent, beautiful young woman washing red peppers in a bucket. I was excited to discover how their love would conquer circumstance, culture, language, class, and nationality. I knew there was a Happy Ever After, or at least a Happy After, because I was sitting with its fruit.

"So anyway, one day, he follows her as she leaves the market to go home. He gets closer and closer to her, and then he grabs her."

"Grabs her?" Evelyn said.

"Grabs her. Drags her behind some trees and rapes her."

I dropped my fork. Evelyn froze.

"UHHM," said Kirsty.

"In those times," Simon continued, "if you'd had sex with a man, you had to marry him. So, she married him. They moved into a small place together. She got pregnant. She got pregnant again. Then again. They had seven children. My mother was the sixth."

"Did they stay together?" I asked, leaning forward so he could see me around Evelyn.

"They were happily married for sixty years. Both died in their late eighties."

"UHHM."

"Makes you wonder, yes?" Robert said. "Or perhaps not? I think yes."

"How do you define *happy*?" Evelyn asked.

"They looked happy. My dad never learnt Malay, so I couldn't ask him."

"Wait, he lived in Malaysia for sixty years but never learnt the language?"

"No. He was quite simple. A fisherman."

My head hurt. "How did they communicate?"

"Gestures mostly. A bit of Malay here. A touch of Japanese there. It was like they had their own special kind of language. It was sweet, really."

"UHHM."

"Aussie, Aussie, Aussie!"

"Oi, Oi, Oi!"

"How do you feel about your grandfather?" Robert asked. "I could imagine you're quite conflicted, yes? He was not a good man, but without him you would not exist?"

Simon paused. "He was my grandfather."

"Yes."

"That's it. I try not to judge. Although when I am feeling judgemental, I hate him, I guess."

"UHHM."

"Do you think she loved him?" Evelyn asked.

"Yes. Or at least she was at peace with him and what he'd done."

No one was sure what to do next. Spoons scraped bowls

and plates. Eye contact became too heavy to hold. The tabletop became immensely fascinating. Simon noticed. "I've sort of killed the mood. I'm sorry. It's good. Worked out fine. They're responsible for at least twenty people existing. Including me." He raised his beer. "To granddads."

It was hard to know what to conclude from this story. How to pack it up and file it away. It directly challenged sentimental notions of fate, destiny, and free will. Had love conquered all? Had lust? Or just power? Did it even matter?

"What was your granddad like?" Evelyn asked me.

"I always meant to write a book about my granddad," I said, laughing. "He was, well, unique. *Yours?*"

"Nice. He sold spices."

24

# DOWN THE RABBIT HOLE

"Evelyn," I said, as we walked the path from the restaurant to the hotel. "Do you want to have kids one day?" She'd seemed very happy holding other people's, from what I'd seen.

"I guess," she said.

"You guess? It's a big decision for guessing, no?"

Her pace slowed. "I mean, yes. *I do*. I suppose. But I'd have to find someone to take on that project with. I have a friend who's a single mum. *No*. Just no. I don't want that for myself. So, I need a guy. A good guy."

"They can't be that hard to find, right?"

"I've never found one. Never even celebrated an anniversary with someone. What are the odds I'll find someone I could imagine spending twenty years raising a kid with? It's like planning a loft extension without owning a house."

"I know what you mean."

"Did you ever come close?"

"Never," I said. "The desire is new."

"You might have," she said.

"What do you mean?"

"Did I tell you about my second boyfriend? James? He was... well... a character. Trouble found James."

*Is she saying I'm not a character? That if trouble found me it would only be to taunt me for being such a square?*

"You never knew what would happen when you were with him, but that fun came at a high price—he was unstable, impulsive, mean. He had ADHD, I think, but undiagnosed. He self-medicated with alcohol.

"Anyway, one day I get this message from him that says, 'I have to go to the USA immediately!' We were off and on by this point. More off than on, really. I asked what the rush was. Now, he'd told me about his first love: a girlfriend he'd had when he was nineteen. She'd become pregnant, and since her parents were Christian, they'd put pressure on them to marry. James had reluctantly agreed, but the relationship was rocky. If you knew James you'd know why. He was rockier than a famous mountain range. Anyway, as the wedding grew closer, they fought more and more. Then her stomach started cramping really badly and so he took her to the emergency room. When he picked her up, she told him the bad news. That she'd miscarried. She then broke up with him and transferred to a university a few states away."

"Wow. Harsh."

"Yep. But... *James*. He didn't think much more about her until..." She raised her hands and smiled. She knew where this was going and was enjoying driving it there.

"One morning he wakes up to a Facebook message from a member of her family. An uncle, I think. She'd been in court the day before fighting a custody battle with her now husband. Her husband was fighting for access to their daughter and she was trying to restrict it. Which she couldn't do. Unless..."

"Oh. Shit," I said, having just worked out the story's destination.

Evelyn winked. "It wasn't his daughter. It was James's. She'd only pretended to have a miscarriage at the hospital, and then she moved away and immediately started dating this other guy. He must have been lousy at math because he didn't notice the timing of the pregnancy was off. They married and raised James's daughter. The one James never knew existed."

I stopped. A shiver worked its way down my spine. This was too much, too upsetting, reminded me of that feeling again—of the overwhelming precariousness of everything. That, one morning, you can sit at the breakfast table with a firm idea of who you are and of what that day will bring. In front of you is the usual morning bowl of muesli. You're mindlessly surfing on your phone and then open Facebook. There you see you have a new message. You scoop up another soggy mouthful of oats and fruit and crunch down on it, cold milk splashing between your lips. You start to read, oblivious to the fact that by the time you've finished chewing, everything will have changed. That this insignificant moment you think you're in is actually monumental. That fate is about to push you down the rabbit hole. That at its bottom you'll blink, confused, looking out on a new reality. One where you've become a father. A father who has missed out on the first nine years of his kid's life. Or one where you're in Kerala racing a tuk-tuk whilst madly in lust. Or one where you're married to your rapist.

We're all memoir writers. All trying hard to rewrite the messy happenstance of our lives into a story that we can live with. One that makes sense to us, more or less. Something neat and linear with clear arcs of progress and achievement. Something that makes us feel in control. That we're not with Alice stumbling lost around Wonderland.

"What did he do?" I asked.

"He booked that flight. He didn't come back. Went to be with his kid."

"How could she?"

"Right."

"Are you still in touch?"

*Please say no.*

"No."

"Might be worth it for the stories."

She laughed.

"We've all got stories," I said, trying to think of anything that could compete with this. What could compete with this? We walked on as I thought back through my previous girlfriends—all kind, reliable, normal. Compared to a life with James, one with me would be impossibly tedious. The only thing I ever forgot was all the embarrassing things I did. I had about as many sharp edges as a bouncy castle. The only thing I self-medicated with was waffles.

Was that going to be enough?

## 25

# RACE DAY THREE: CALICUT TO MANGALORE

It was 6am again. Why was it always 6am? In the hotel lobby, Evelyn passed me the breakfast biscuits and a carton of orange juice.

"Morning, you lovely, lovely idiots," said Aarav. He was in a good mood, which was the only thing more annoying than when he was in a bad mood. "So, yesterday, despite all our best efforts, only two of you arrived after sundown and lost all your points." He pinched his nose. "This is obviously too easy. Next year we're going to halve the time and remove a wheel from each rickshaw. *The front wheel*." He cackled. "The front wheel!"

Pamir nodded solemnly, dark clouds swirling in his mind; rain was forecast in there.

"Today has some more horrible roads. And just wait for Mangalore. It's not a city, it's a city-sized traffic jam. Oh, I've forgotten one thing haven't I, Pamir?"

"You have," Pamir said, blowing his word budget for the day.

"We've added another thirty kilometres to yesterday's drive."

The group groaned as Aarav licked his lips. "Oh, how I love to make you groan. Today you'll drive 258 kilometres! Longest stretch of the whole week. Now, yesterday, we had one crash. It was team..." His eyes rolled upwards.

"The Tuk-Tuk Trolls," said Pamir.

"Right. At lunchtime their brakes were feeling spongy. Now, did they tell us? Did they call? Send a text? Shoot up a flare? *No*." He hung his head. "It's hard not to take that personally, isn't it, Pamir?"

"Sure is."

"They kept driving. They're not here. Are they, Pamir?"

"They're not. They're dead."

A pause as they scanned our faces to see if we'd bought into their lie.

"Yeah... DEAD late!" Aarav said, firing shots from twin finger guns. "See what I did there?"

*They must choreograph these routines.*

"They're still at breakfast. They were coming down a hill and their brakes failed. Scariest moment of their lives, they said. Crashed into the back of a car, they did. Smashed their little rickshaw up good too. Real scene, it was. Wasn't it, Pamir?"

"Real scene."

"So, anyway, moral of the story? If your brakes feel spongy, stop. Actually, possibly the moral is don't sign up for stupid challenges like this." Aarav slapped his thigh. "Too late!"

---

"I have an official announcement to make," I said. "I was a bit sad when my last driving shift ended."

"That's quite a statement."

"I stand behind it."

Evelyn considered it for a few steps. "You know, I think I'm also hating it less and less."

"Could you be more enthusiastic?"

"Yes."

"It's a start, I guess."

We were making such good time we'd veered off into the pretty coastal city of Kochi to visit its famous old town. Given that there'd been little traffic on the road and our confidence in handling the tuk-tuk's quirks was growing, it had been an exquisite drive. We hadn't stalled even once as we followed the coastal roads and zipped over causeways past fishermen tending to brightly coloured nets and boats with chipped paint.

It would be easy to misrepresent the scenery of Kerala, to sell it as an endless vista of outstanding natural beauty. Beautiful it was; in part. But most of the tuk-tuk race experience wasn't gazing lovingly down from romantic bridges, plucking figs from the tendons of majestic trees, or drinking sweet, milky tea in the shaded gardens of new friends caught in our net of foreignness.

No, it was bouncing down the unpaved roads of forgettable, scruffy towns, wincing at twinges in our lower backs, fighting off relentless attacks on what little space we snatched for ourselves, coughing into the toxic exhaust of rusty buses, and wondering when the next traffic jam would subject us to a tedious, indefinite period of Waiting.

I'd now been to enough of the world to know that most places aren't beautiful. Aren't memorable. Aren't destinations, even. The only tourism they see is economic: trucks, cars, and lorries there to drop off, pick up, and pass people through.

They're in-between places visited by in-between people.

Fortunately, Kochi was not an in-between place. It was a destination. A pretty jewel—but that brings its own problems.

People like jewels. The British, Dutch, and Portuguese fought over this one for a hundred years because owning it meant controlling Kerala's lucrative spice trade. Where Evelyn and I now stood, countries had taken turns conquering and blowing up each other's sacred buildings. This strip had once been a thriving Jewish community. It was now a single street, Jew Street, which ended in the synagogue built here in 1760.

We strolled amiably, feigning an unhurried air as we passed souvenir shops, spice merchants, and the last few antique shops that had also once made the area famous. It was joyous to be out of the tuk-tuk, off the road, and walking with the illusion of time—and the chance to talk in more than shouted snatches of conversation.

"Have you noticed how your focus has changed, compared to day one?" Evelyn asked. "Back in Trivandrum, driving was like playing a computer game called EVERYONE IS SUICIDAL EXCEPT ME. But now? The..." She considered the right wording. I prepared for another unique Evelyn construct. "The Zone of Concern keeps narrowing. Now I only look behind me when overtaking. Everything has sort of become everyone else's problem."

"Perfect description of my world view. To be honest, I no longer even notice I'm driving. It's just kind of instinct." I stopped. "Wait. That means I have... *driving instincts*?"

We high-fived. Immersion therapy works wonderfully. That Alsatian and I were now best buds. *My fear was cured.* And I'd also changed my mind about something else: before the trip, I'd always been deeply suspicious of people who did driving holidays. Weren't you more likely to meet people when not in a glass-and-metal bubble engineered precisely to keep them out? Wasn't nature easier to appreciate at walking speed?

I was wrong. The tuk-tuk thrust us into conversation wherever we went. We were roving celebrities discovering what it was like to *be* Stanley Tucci and a young Bette Midler, whoever she was. Forward momentum—the dull thud of the earth below the tyres as the kilometres disappeared beneath us—was deeply satisfying. I would do a driving holiday again. Just not with these kinds of distances. And maybe somewhere with more respect for road rules. And a few hundred million people fewer, perhaps.

We turned the corner and there, waiting, seemingly smiling at us, was the tuk-tuk. "You know, I think it's time we named it."

Evelyn stopped and stared at it, her head slowly tilting. "How about Winnie?"

"Winnie," I said slowly. "Perfect. I think I'm kind of falling for the girl."

"It's a girl?"

"Obviously."

"Why?"

"Just feels like a woman to me. It's small, delicate, temperamental, changes gears erratically."

"You don't know much about women, do you?"

"I thought this would have been obvious by now?"

## 26

## DODO IDEAS

I don't want to alarm you, but I think you should know. Every second of the day, somewhere, a meeting is taking place. In it, a hand is going up. The room is turning to the owner of that hand. That person is clearing their throat. "Err, so I've had this one idea," they say, almost apologetically, as they shuffle open a yellow manila folder.

There are no bad ideas in brainstorming, right?

*Wrong*. Bad ideas are everywhere. The world is literally drowning in crud. It's neck-deep and sinking in nincompoop.

The only reason you should sleep soundly at night is because, in this complex, chaotic world, there are many, many gatekeepers between you and all the terrible proposals, hare-brained schemes, stinker notions, intellectual own goals, and Dodo Ideas being proposed by people with raised hands.

They might be silenced directly: with a shake of the head, a reminder of the rules, a "you can't be serious," a "we tried that already," a "think how much that would cost." Or indirectly: with a swift "let's sleep on it," a deftly weighted "*interesting*," or a firm "we'll get back to you."

This is precisely why it's so disconcerting when we come

face-to-face with a Dodo Idea in the wild, running amok through people's lives, whether it's airport security, the rabbit-proof fence, the Berlin Wall, the mullet, the five-day workweek, Piers Morgan, or kombucha. For it shows that the gauntlet between hand raise and everyday life is not as fiercely protected as we thought. That a Dodo can slip through and out into the world and stink it up like a dog's fart in an elevator.

It was because of one of these ideas that Evelyn and I had lost the last hour of our lives in a really long queue at a bank.

In November 2016, some six months before we arrived in India, the country's prime minister, Narendra Modi, appeared on TV to announce—having given no prior warning, not even to his own cabinet—that the vast majority of the country's paper money would become useless in just fifty days' time. "Demonetisation," he called it. "Demo" for short. But it was no demo—it was live, unstoppable, to affect all 15.4 trillion ₹500 and ₹1,000 banknotes. These had to be swapped at banks for new ₹500 notes and ₹2,000 notes. This would help curtail the shadow economy, reduce illegal activity, and curtailing the funding of terrorism.

Or so he said.

Cash is king, queen, rook, bishop, and knight in India. At any moment you can stop in the street, swing your gaze left and right, and observe these precious, dirty, moulding, folded, rectangular lumps of pure government-backed potential skimming between hands like stones across a lake: paying for bumpy taxi rides; plastic bags heaving with groceries; life-giving medicine; life-changing dowries; life-enriching jewellery; sex, slumber, and saffron. They are the petrol in the great capitalist engine of progress that is the Indian economy.

The government held off from printing much of this new money in advance. After Modi's announcement, there was a frantic rush—people emptied their piggy banks, safes, coffee tins, and mattress slits and took their savings to banks only to find there were no new banknotes waiting for them there. Those lines grew long. So long, in fact, that there were a few deaths in them and quite a spike in suicides as people panicked. Money works on belief, and belief was a currency the government was now also lacking in. The clock ticked on regardless. Fifty days became forty. Then thirty.

Slowly, painfully, inefficiently, the new money arrived. By the deadline, 99.3% of the demonetised banknotes had been exchanged. If the bad guys were stashing notes, they seemingly had no problem removing them from their hiding places and converting them. While it was too early to call the initiative completely pointless, it had certainly crippled the country's booming GDP and harmed the reputation of its beleaguered prime minister. Six months later, the lines weren't as long, but there was still a shortage of those new notes.

India has had more than its fair share of Dodo Ideas—many instigated by the East India Company or the British Raj. To understand India's messy present, and the fractious relationship it has with its neighbours, and why it has those neighbours at all, there's another Dodo Idea you need to know about: the Radcliffe Line.

Remember our story of the East India Company? The David that became a Goliath? The company that took over an empire?

They're back in England now. The British Raj has moved into their old forts and homes. They've been there for a hundred years or so when they get a telegram from Blighty. Trouble in Europe. Tricky situation with a certain Herr Hitler. Could the Raj slap a gun or two over the arms of some of its servants, sorry, *subjects*, and send them over to help?

Raj was happy to; people he had. He rounded up two-and-a-half million Indian soldiers, and with their help, Britain won the Second World War. But the cost devastated the British

Empire, and they could no longer afford to administer India. And anyway, colonies were becoming frowned upon.

So, they decided on a deadline of June 1948 to return it to self-governance. But whose governance? The country was split on sectarian lines between the approximately 75% Hindu population and the 25% Muslim. Some, like Ghandi, wanted a one-state solution, while others—particularly the minority Muslim population—pushed for their own state: Pakistan. There was a lot of squabbling. Raj listened to some of it but got distracted by thoughts of the troubles back home. He brought the deadline forward to August 1947, which killed diplomacy and tipped the favour towards a two-state solution. But the Muslim and Hindu populations were not neatly arranged in geographic blocks that could be made to fall logically over some new groove in a map. Regardless, the British sent someone to decide where to scratch this new border into the dirt.

They gave him just seven weeks to do so. They really did have a lot going on. The man sent was Cyril Radcliffe. He'd never been to India before. And they gave him out-of-date maps and census data. Still, he did the job. Or *a* job. Once finished, the Radcliffe Line split the country into two administrative parts: India and Pakistan. Pakistan was then further divided into two illogical and hard-to-govern sections separated by 1,700 kilometres. The eastern part would later be reborn as Bangladesh, some twenty-five years hence.

Cyril left the next day. Said he worried they'd shoot him otherwise. Prudent, for in his wake began perhaps the bloodiest, most harrowing human migrations ever recorded: fifteen million people uprooted, moving on foot, in carts, and on trains, all trying to reach a region where their faith would be majority. So, Muslims towards this new Pakistan and Hindus towards India. On the way, they met each other. Muslims hunted Hindus and Sikhs, Hindus and Sikhs hunted Muslims.

Between one and two million people were murdered as roads became impassably littered with the dead.

What begins with a raise of an arm and the clearing of a throat matters. For while ideas might be simple, the world never, ever is. Our line, the one ending at the ATM, shuffled forwards—the money had arrived.

27

# THE MECHANIC

"Favourite book?" Evelyn asked. We were being held captive at the edge of a large roundabout. How long had we been driving? *Twelve hours? Thirteen?* At least we were now in Mangalore.

"Anything by Will Storr."

"Who's that?"

"Non-fiction guy. Writes about beliefs and where we get our weird ones from, mostly."

You knew things were bad here when the people idling in traffic turned off their engines. Everyone had turned off their engines.

"You don't read fiction?"

"Rarely."

"You?"

"Chimamanda Ngozi Adichie."

"Come again?"

"Nigerian feminist."

"Ten a penny."

"What?"

"Nigerian feminists."

"What about Nigerian feminists?

"Never mind." I pounded the steering column in frustration. "Oh, come on! What are we even waiting for?" I was dreaming of cold beer, hot food, and an early bedtime. The sun was retreating from the sky in a practised manoeuvre called dusk. Day three had stretched more than an octogenarian before a marathon. It had felt like a marathon. Our pockets bulged with cash we'd have no time to spend as we fed each other biscuits and spicy peanut snacks and chatted the hours away in Winnie.

In the hostage negotiation that is Indian traffic, you rarely know how long you'll be held. Then, suddenly, as if all the abducted decide collectively they can't take it anymore, everyone switches on their engines and surges forwards together.

"Wanna swap?" she asked. Traffic jams were the hardest on Evelyn's wrists because they involved much delicate clutch and biting-point work to avoid stalling Winnie's sensitive engine. Each evening her wrist would swell to the size of a golf ball.

"No, it's fine," I said, suppressing how I really felt, which was like yoghurt left in the sun to curdle.

*Wait a second... Was that...? Yes.*

Hands dropped. Phones disappeared into pockets. Noise.

*We're moving. MOVING!*

What had delayed us? We'd never know.

Just enough of the roundabout cleared for me to fight my way in, honking, revving, letting people know I wasn't here to play. That they were between my well-earned recreation and me. I barged into each tiny gap until, once again, as on day one, Evelyn and I had a choice: we could go right and follow a bridge over a river into the city, or descend left down a road that curled back under that bridge along the shoreline.

"Bridge or slip road?" I asked.

"We're out of Internet again. I think... *bridge*?"

And so, we soared above another lazy river and followed a few bends until we were spat unceremoniously into the loudly beating heart of the city's central bazaar. In rush hour. Everyone and everything that existed was here spilling from stall fronts and shops. You wanted it? They had it. You didn't want it? They had it anyway.

Things that lit up.

Things you blew.

Things that whistled.

Things you threw.

Things that lit up when you blew, whistled, and threw them. If China had thought of it, it was falling from the tops of brown cardboard boxes hosting orgies of shrink-wrapped plastic.

"There's no way they'd have booked us a hotel this central," I said, fighting off a scooter for thirty centimetres of space behind a slowly advancing truck. "We're not in places long enough."

That runaway-mine-train of a headache was back and racing at breakneck speeds through the tunnels of my mind.

"Ohhhhhh," Evelyn said, having won the latest bout with her phone. "So, funny story, turns out it was left. *Damn*. The hotel was just around that bend."

This was not a funny story. It was a sad, tragic story, like that one where the plane crashed into the mountain and people had to eat each other. We had crashed into the free market and now it would gobble up our whole evening. Irritation pummelled each of my organs. I felt like life and I were playing whack-a-mole. And there was only one hole. And I was the mole.

I continued manipulating the clutch and accelerator, maintaining the delicate engine-harmony required to keep us edging forwards. I was fed up, and fed up with always being fed up through days dominated by driving and little else. But there was nowhere to turn around on this narrow road of snarled-up traffic.

A scooter squeezed alongside, its mirror knocking into mine. "Selfie?"

I looked at its driver. "No."

I tried to nudge us forwards, but at that moment, the engine cut out.

*No. Not here. Anywhere but here.*

I moved to neutral and pumped the lever. Nothing.

I fumbled with the controls. I knew neutral, could have found its tiny notch in the dark, blindfolded, with my teeth. We were blocking the road. There was space yet we were not filling it. This was unthinkable. Unforgivable. The honking was a wild, ravenous, all-compassing thing. An orchestra of annoyance. A symphony of dissatisfaction. A ballad of betrayal.

The horns brought the people.

They stopped shopping.

They turned.

They whispered.

They stared. Staring isn't a provocation here. With so many people everywhere, at all times, Indians seemed to accept that privacy was like a solid gold toilet: nice in theory but unaffordable. And if you're always being watched by someone, does it really matter exactly how many someones? Everyone's gaze fell onto us—the idiot white people pretending they knew how to drive a tuk-tuk, cluttering up the bazaar with their flagrant incompetence.

My movements were rapid and panicked as I wiped sweat from my eyebrows and repeated the starting process a final time.

It was no use. I spun around. "We've broken down!"

Evelyn knew that already. I found her struggling for breath, gulping like a water-boarded kitten. "There!" she said, pointing to a narrow alleyway up ahead, between two rows of the market; just wide enough for us. She leapt out and began shoving Winnie forwards as five locals jumped alongside. "We are pushing?"

She nodded. "We are pushing."

Nudging scooters aside, we soon reached the alley, where she orchestrated a three-point turn so we could enter backwards. I got out and leaned against Winnie's frame trying to calm my nerves as people swarmed around us. "What's the problem, boss?" a man in sunglasses asked.

"Broken down?" said another man.

"Where are you going?" enquired a third.

"Where are you from?" asked a fourth.

"Selfie?" said a fifth.

"We know mechanic," said the first. "He is coming."

It was too much. I bent over, sucking large gulps of air. When I resurfaced, another two dozen people had appeared to jam the alley with helpers and rubberneckers. Someone had slipped past me into the driver's seat and three people were round the back. They had the engine hatch open and were prodding things and shouting at the man in the front seat.

"Mechanic come soon," someone said, as I got out my phone and called Pamir.

"Pamir, we've broken down."

He let out a long sigh. It was the terrible news he'd been expecting. "Where?"

"Well, we sort of got lost and accidentally drove into downtown Mangalore. We're at the central bazaar."

I heard him translating for someone. "Not good. Is the tuk-tuk okay?"

I'd hoped for a little more concern about us. "Yeah, it just won't start."

"It's rush hour. I don't know how long it will take us to get there."

"Some people are here and they're helping."

"Okay, put one of them on." There are over a thousand languages spoken in India—more than a hundred widely so. Pamir and the man tested several to see which they had in common; language speed-dating. Remarkably, they couldn't find one, so the man passed the phone on, and the process was repeated until a suitable match was found. How did anything get done in this country?

A few minutes went by as the man and his helpers poked around in the motor but failed to get Winnie going again. This was bad. Especially since Juliane and Evelyn had decided not to buy the extra breakdown package, which meant we were liable for all repair costs.

"Pamir's on his way," I said.

"How'd he take it?" Evelyn asked.

"Like a hammer to the heart."

The crowd whispered...

Then it parted...

I turned towards the market and saw a man sitting, his legs folded under him in the lotus position, on an adapted silver skateboard of some kind. He was pulling himself down the road on his hands, teeth gritted. He stopped at the opening of the alley, leaned on the right side of the skateboard to turn, and made two more valiant pulls towards me.

"Mechanic," whispered the people.

The man hewobbled as he passed, shooing people away, and settled himself at the engine. He got to work surrounding himself with as many of its screws, nuts, and bolts as possible before identifying a length of orange tubing that he particularly liked. He blew on it as though it were a novelty trumpet.

To be part of this scene was agony. Here we were in a culture we didn't understand, racing a vehicle we didn't know how to drive, blocking traffic trying to get home, and making a poor disabled mechanic on a silver skateboard pull himself around with his bare hands and blow in orange tubes as though they were novelty trumpets.

Several minutes passed. They were long and laced with severity.

*Is it our fault?*
*Will we lose the €1000 deposit we paid for Winnie?*
*Will we need to drop out of the race?*
*Will we need a new engine?*
*How long will we be stuck here?*

Then… a shout! I turned to the mechanic, who beamed a smile back at me. He'd found the problem. It had taken all his years of training and expertise.

*What is it? And how serious?*

He shouted something. I braced myself and turned to the man in sunglasses for a translation. The man laughed.

*Why is he laughing?*

Now everyone was laughing!

*Why is everyone laughing?*

"You've run out of petrol," he said. A rash of embarrassment broke out across my body, and I silently begged the world to swallow me up. This would be the first incident in my worst-of reel, I realised, as I walked to Winnie's back shelf, removed the two litres of emergency petrol, and handed them down to him.

All this fuss for nothing. I wanted out of here. I wanted a cold shower. I wanted to be far enough into the future that this was just a funny anecdote, a story I'd told so often that I no longer felt it. The mechanic propelled himself forwards on closed fists and stopped at the driver's seat. I thanked him and went to climb in. He gestured me back with a flick of his hand, then grabbed the vehicle's frame and hoisted himself into the front seat, where he unfurled his lower limbs and wedged them down onto the pedals.

*Why is he doing this? Is it hurting him to do this?*

He pulled nonchalantly on the starter lever and the engine coughed awake. He then did some things that were not obvious to me. It looked as if he did nothing much, really—merely twisted the accelerator to rev the engine, rubbed his head a lot, revved the engine more, and scratched at his ratty beard. But he did all these things with great ceremony and showmanship, as if he were the star of a one-man play entitled *I Will Save the Day*.

I was sure we were out of the woods. That everything was fine now. Yet he acted otherwise. As if we were actually just one wrong turn away from getting so lost in the woods of ineptitude that we'd end up in the oven of a woman whose house was made of gingerbread.

The crowd watched on, enraptured. I folded in on myself, embarrassed.

*Where's Evelyn?*

I looked around and spotted her behind the tuk-tuk. Two schoolgirls in purple-and-white uniforms were touching her hair and complimenting it. Eventually, the mechanic sat back in the seat, a self-satisfied smile on his face, and gave one strong, slow nod. He grabbed the frame of the tuk-tuk and swung himself down, plopping back onto his skateboard. There, he curled his legs back under himself and did a final, ceremonial hewobble.

The fifty people watching let out a cheer. I pulled the biggest note from my wallet and thrust it in his direction. In that moment, in my heightened state of awkwardness, I'd have given him all the money I had in the world. Awkwardness; here it was again.

The mechanic nudged the money back towards me. Surely he'd done this for money? I insisted and pushed it forwards, only for him to push it back.

*What was I not getting? Why wouldn't he take it?*

I edged it back towards him, but he batted it away then

dropped his fists to the mud and rolled himself away. This wasn't about money. It was about pride. He had saved us.

What a hero.

That hero melted into the throng of the market. I circled, thanking everyone profusely. We were free. As I was thanking them, I noticed my arms were shaking uncontrollably and my eyes refused to focus. It was like looking at the world through the bottom of a glass bottle.

Until this moment, I'd said "my nerves are shot" many times, without truly knowing what the phrase meant. I now knew. "Evelyn? Your meet-and-greet over?"

"Yes. Sorry," she said, handing back a baby to someone. "Such lovely people."

"Got a few more life stories?"

"Yep. And four offers to host us if we're ever back in town. Or get stuck forever in the town."

"Do you think you can drive us out of here?"

She looked at the tuk-tuk, then at me. It was still my shift. "Yeah, sure."

"Thank you." I climbed into the back before she had time to change her mind, and because it was much easier to hide there.

Evelyn moved towards the driver's seat. This sent the crowd whirling in disbelief, sniggers, and double takes. Phones were pulled from pockets for the recording of evidence. A woman driving a tuk-tuk? A white woman? With blonde hair? Ridiculous. Until then they'd assumed she was just my glamorous assistant.

She climbed in. She was going to be ridiculous.

The mechanic had left the engine running. She tickled the accelerator and stared out at the Tetris blocks of traffic shifting and rotating to fill every centimetre of road. By this point, deep into day three, Evelyn was a good, albeit safe, driver. However, just like Superman, she had a kryptonite of a flaw:

she was paranoid about turning sharply. It had started when we saw Lance flip his tuk-tuk. The alleyway met the road at an unforgiving ninety-degree angle. It was a narrow road, and it had just one lane for left-hand traffic. "You can do this. When we go, *hard left*, okay?"

"Okay," she shouted, staring out into the traffic with a steely look of determination. "Hard left. Okay! Let's go!"

We waited for a gap. "NOW! HARD LEFT. HARD LEFT!" We shot forwards, Evelyn wrenching the controls as hard and as left as her flimsy, swollen wrists allowed.

"LEFT LEFT LEFT LEFT LEFT LEFT!" she screamed as we entered the road, turning, turning, turning. A lorry approached from the opposite direction, crowding the space we needed, its right wing mirror looming ever closer.

I closed my eyes. I heard the crowd cheer. I slowly opened them. We were out. We were on the road. Evelyn had done it. She'd saved us.

I turned and waved goodbye to our new friends.

We were away.

We were fine.

We were a team. A damn good one.

We would survive this.

But then what...?

28

## THE HOTEL ROOM

"That was the longest day of my entire life," I said, as we drove the long path that ran alongside the hotel to the car park hidden behind it. We were so late that no one was there to wave a black-and-white chequered flag for us. We'd missed sundown and had thereby forfeited the day's points and some of our measly recreation hours.

As I removed the bags from the tuk-tuk, Evelyn held up her wrist. "It looks like I fought an elephant and lost."

I dropped the bags, nudged her arm aside, and hugged her. "Thank you."

"For what?"

"You saved us." As we came apart, I felt her good hand linger for longer than necessary on my lower back.

"Pff," she said. "It was nothing."

"What do you want to do tonight?" I asked.

"I want to drink two glasses of wine then pass out. We're late for the group dinner, right?"

"Yeah, and I need to see if they've got a free room for me."

"Stay in mine," she said. Her tongue came to rest between her teeth.

"Did you know it was a double bed?" I asked, as the door closed behind us.

"They never asked," she said. Which meant she'd not specified that it shouldn't be, which meant she might not care that it shouldn't be. *Which couldn't mean... could it?*

She looked at the bedside clock. "What time did we say we'd meet the others?"

"Eight."

"It's 8:15. I have to quickly shower. I look like a coal miner." She dropped her backpack and swerved off into the bathroom. I stood in the middle of the room, afraid to touch anything because I'd smother it with grime but not wanting to remove my clothes because then I'd be there not in my clothes. I pulled the chair from the desk and sat on it, waiting for my turn to shower.

---

The restaurant was on the building's top floor and had a terrace that provided an unparalleled view of Mangalore's many motorways.

"Why are you two lovebirds late?" Manish grinned. "Like we don't know."

Evelyn blushed.

"Breakdown," I said.

"Sure," said Sonia, with a slow, theatrical wink. "If that's what the kids are calling it now."

They were sitting next to each other, their backs to the wall, looking out towards the street. I went to sit opposite Sonia, then decided Evelyn would probably want to, but by then I'd already pulled out the chair. I left it and crossed to the other chair, which made it look like I'd pulled out the first chair for her, which was weird, because it was 2017 and not 1817. Manish whistled. "We've got ourselves a gentleman here, ladies and, erm... *gentlemen*."

"Not too gentle though, I hope?" said Sonia, scratching at the air like a cat.

"Can you two leave it out?"

"More like can you leave it out?" Manish quipped, and the two of them collapsed into contagious laughter.

"So how was your day?" I asked, trying to change the subject. As they finished their meals, they described a day very much like our own, minus the breakdown. Evelyn and I then did our first duet of that story. At one point, Evelyn was out of her chair and scooting around on an imaginary silver skateboard as Manish wiped away tears of laughter.

Wine flowed. It wasn't good wine—this country didn't speak its language yet—but it was potent wine, and that was more than enough. With it, the edges of the world melted as if held over a candle's flame.

Two hours later, to speed things up, I told Evelyn I'd pay the bill and headed to the cashier.

"Good, sir?" the cashier asked.

"Wonderful," I said, giddy on the wine, the conversation, the friendship, and the knowledge that Evelyn and I would go back to one room and one bed. I turned from the counter to see Evelyn looking over at me, a wide, inviting grin on that perfect face.

"Oh, come on," I heard Sonia saying, as I walked back towards the table. "I've seen how you two look at each other."

*Were they talking about me? About us?*

I paused to see how Evelyn would respond, but she'd already seen me. Sonia turned and closed her mouth, and as she did, the subject dropped to the floor and crawled off into the past.

The four of us walked the few streets back to the hotel

talking, laughing, and narrowly avoiding being run over at each junction. It seemed just as dangerous to be a pedestrian here as a tuk-tuk racer. And then there was an entrance and stairs and a corridor and a goodnight and a just-us and a door and a key and a sense building within me that this might be one of those really, really rare moments when someone in the world actually gets what they want.

And that I might be that someone.

And then even that door was behind us.

And then there was just a bed.

And this time, clean, I climbed onto it as Evelyn disappeared once more into the bathroom. The air in the room was so charged that it seemed to dart madly around me, smashing into things, as I lay down on my back, waiting for her. Soon she'd be out. Should I do something? Or let her make the first move? Could I encourage that move, somehow? How should I be sitting when she returned? I needed to strike the right pose: casual, a touch suggestive, but with no hint of ambush. A delicate balance was required, and I was almost certainly too drunk to hold it.

I turned the light on. *No, too bright.*

I turned the light off. *No, too dark.*

I turned the lamp on. *Better.* Both lamps? *Better better.*

Should I face her? Or lie on my back? I turned towards the bathroom then returned to my back, becoming a rotating kebab of indecision. What about facing her, resting on one elbow? Classy, the one elbow.

The toilet flushed. She was coming, and I didn't even have a prototype position yet. THERE WAS NO TIME. I propped myself up on one elbow, my head resting on my palm.

*Ugh.* It wasn't classy at all. It was pompous and try-hard. *Quick, think...* What said casual but suggestive without the hint of ambush?

The bathroom lock disengaged. I sat up and crossed my

legs, dropped my hands casually on my thighs, and straightened my back; strong, confident. It had really come together, and with not a second to spare.

The door opened. She stepped out, then stopped. "You okay there?"

"Sure."

"What you doing? Yoga?" Her tone was tinged with mirth.

I looked down at myself. "Err. *Yes*?" I said, trying to cover up the fact that I'd accidentally adopted a Buddhist power stance of enlightenment. It was suggestive, but suggested I was soaring high on a plane of existence well above base carnal desires like sex. Which couldn't have been further from the truth.

A rectangular pocket of light burst into the room as her phone awoke. It lay between us on the bed, all sharp edges and cold metallic arrogance, knowing full well it could take her from me whenever it wanted. That it was my true rival, not Lance. She scooped it up. "Oh no," she said, as it pinged once more. "Oh, shit."

"What?"

"Terror attack in Germany. Every news site will want a statement immediately."

The phone rang, and it did so smugly. In my stomach, an elevator packed full of hope and excitement snapped and plunged down. "But you won't even really know what's happened yet, right?"

She held up her finger. "Hey. Yeah, I've seen," she said in German, as worry lines tiptoed across her forehead. "No, it's fine. The race is over for today. Yeah, we need to draft something *straight away*." She pulled on her sandals and walked towards the door. "Can you talk to..." She stepped out, and the door closed behind her.

I dropped my power stance of enlightenment and flumped down onto the bed, releasing all the oxygen I'd trapped in my chest in the hope it might make me look like a fearsome warrior instead of a frightened wimp.

This was a strange situation, and I felt conflicted. Did I have the right to be annoyed? I mean, people had probably died. That was much more important than my getting laid. Are you allowed to be irritated at the timing of a terror attack? Aren't they, by definition, always inconvenient? And I had to respect that she had an important job. People depended on her.

But...

Well...

Still...

I mean...

REALLY? RIGHT NOW?

I stared up at the ceiling. The fan whirled above me. It couldn't take that long to prepare a statement, could it?

## 29

# RACE DAY FOUR: MANGALORE TO MURUDESHWAR

I still don't know how long it takes to prepare a statement because I didn't hear her come to bed. It must have been late, because I waited a long time, staring first at the ceiling and then at my Kindle as hope grew stooped, haggard, and frail. Finally, I shoved it off to a possibility retirement home to die bitter and full of what-could-have-been.

"Morning, you ugly mugs," said Aarav. "Day four? Let me say that again. DAY FOUR! It's going so fast, isn't it?"

He couldn't have been more wrong. He searched our faces for excitement. It was 7am. Perhaps he'd hoped the extra hour of sleep would raise our spirits.

He'd hoped in vain.

"Yesterday was the big one." He held his hands out as if measuring a long sausage. "We had *several* breakdowns. Go easy on your little rickshaws, okay? Take some chai breaks. Bloody lovely, the chai here. Let those engines cool a bit." He brought his hands together. "Today, we're going easy on you. Nice roads and a paltry 170 kilometres to cover. Nothing, really, is it? You could throw a stone that far. Don't, though.

You can't throw a stone in this country without hitting twenty-seven people. Two highlights today, right, Pamir?"

Pamir sucked in what he was 50 percent sure was his last breath.

"The first stop is Udupi," Aarav continued. "Cracking little temple there. Then on to Murudeshwar, which is perhaps the highlight of the whole trip. An enormous Shiva awaits. How big, Pamir?"

"Big."

"Sure is. Drive well and you'll see my chequered flag by midafternoon—plenty of time for a cold beer and a swim. Get going then, you horrible lot!"

---

It was the most beautiful cow I'd ever seen. But it was also the only cow I'd ever seen in full makeup. Blood-red and marigold-yellow paint had been smeared on its face. Draped over its shoulders was a tasselled gold cloth. From the sides of its face hung a flower garland, strung from a small copper pot full of green leaves sitting high on its forehead.

It was ready for its closeup.

It was ready for the big time.

It was ready for its wedding day.

I wanted to giggle. I would not giggle. "Cowwwwwwww," said the earnest young man leading the poor animal towards me on a thin, lank rope. The cow looked resigned to its fate, while the young man seemed still open to fighting his.

"Cowwwwwwww," he repeated, in a high-pitched, scratchy tone. "Sacred."

"Yes." *Where were you on day two?* I thought. *When we were dropping crisp packets on beloved pets.* The man shook the tin in his hand, causing the few coins within it to rattle.

"Cowwwwwwww." *Rattle rattle.*

"*Yes.*"

We'd arrived in Udupi and had parked near the famous Sri Krishna Matha temple. I turned from the man to its imposing entrance and stared up, slack mouthed, at the two enormous pillars holding up an ornate carved arch of roaring elephants, bucking horses, a dancing skeleton, and several gods I felt shame for not knowing the names of.

*Rattle rattle.* "Cow!"

I dragged Evelyn towards the entrance before things got so awkward with Mr Cow that she'd hand him her life savings. Assuming she had savings. I hoped she had savings. Someone would have to put our unborn children through college. I'd chosen to become a writer, which was like getting to decide which animal you'd like to be and choosing to be a naked mole rat.

She stopped me at the final step before the temple's entrance. "You can't go in. You're in shorts."

"That's okay."

"It's rude is what it is."

"Your face is rude!" I knocked her hand away. "It'll be fine. Or they'll tell me off. Or give me a wrappy thing. Either way, *fine.*"

She pulled me back by the hand. "What's the point in visiting a culture if you're not going to be respectful of it?"

"I'm respectful... *in shorts*."

"Do you go to temples when you travel?"

"I did at the start."

"And now?"

"*Eh*. I've been in about a thousand, I guess."

"Museums then?"

I shook my head. "They've got too many pots in them, I find. There's nothing worse than turning a corner and seeing a whole room full of big old pots. I don't think there's anyone in the world who's interested in pots. Not even potmakers."

"I think they're called potterers."

"Don't distract me, I'm on a rant. Have you been to the national museum in Beijing? It's about the size of Wales but just pots, pots, pots. So many pots." I tried to mime a pot as big as Wales.

"Probably because of the Ming dynasty," she said. "They made some of the most exquisite, ornate ceramics the world has ever seen. And back in what, like, the fifteenth century?"

She was showing off. "Yeah, as I said, *pots*."

We began traversing the outer square of the temple's courtyard. "I think I'm not really that interested in the past," I said.

She stopped. "Are we just going to let that sentence pass? Or should we, I don't know, unpack it a bit? Decide if it's the most stupid thing anyone's ever said, or merely one of?"

I sucked in my cheeks. "I mean, I like the '90s a bit."

"The 1890s?"

"The 1990s. They had some good music. Before that? It was mostly just pots and smallpox."

Along with the train network, the development of the smallpox vaccination was the other oft-cited high point of the British Raj. Evelyn's hands dropped to her sides. "I don't know whether to envy you or feel sorry for you."

"I like the future, though. It's got all this potential in it, you know? I like how little time it's had to disappoint."

"This a Peak Theory thing?"

I shrugged. A man stopped to greet us. His palm was wrapped over a large curved stick. A red bindi sat between his thick, greying eyebrows. His head was freshly shaved and his eyes burned with sincerity, giving him a wizardly quality.

"Hello," he said.

"Hello."

He angled his face away from us. "Tourists?"

"Yes." That was obvious, wasn't it?

"Welcome."

"Thanks."

"I'm a sanyāsī," he said. "It's like a monk."

"That must be nice," Evelyn said.

"Yes. What do you think of the temple?"

"Lovely," I said. We'd barely looked at it. "A good temple. A fine temple. No pots."

"Pots?"

Evelyn slapped me on the arm. "Never mind."

"Where are you from?"

"Germany," I said, because I knew this wasn't technically true and so would annoy her and we all have to get our kicks somehow.

"No, you're not," she said. "He's English."

"I don't look like it," I said. "I know."

He didn't comment on how I looked, which was a nice change.

"Are you from Udupi?" she asked. He answered, and as he did, I felt myself drift like smoke up from the flames of the conversation, wondering how many times I'd been in one like it somewhere in the world. I didn't mind. Almost all wonderful experiences while travelling follow conversations with *where are you from* openings; they're the entrance ticket to the Circus of Novel Experience. During these conversations, my job is to ask the right questions, show humility and interest, and smile enough to show I have all my teeth. If I'm lucky, this will convince the person I'm hinged. That it's safe to invite me somewhere. That time spent with me will pay them a worthwhile dividend. I wondered how this particular conversation might end. Would we receive handshakes and a "have a nice trip"? Be lavished with hospitality in a modest family home with pet goats? Drink moonshine at a raucous three-day wedding? Dance as extras at the back of a Bollywood movie scene? Or tour a museum full of pots as big as Wales?

Everything felt possible, and that's the feeling travellers cherish most.

I drifted back down.

"No," the man said. "I'm from New Delhi."

"Is there an Old Delhi?" Evelyn asked. "You only ever hear about New Delhi."

"Yes. There's an Old Delhi. It's a walled area inside of Delhi."

"Huh," she said.

"Do you know about Hinduism?" he asked. "It's the oldest religion in the world."

Ah... so that was where this was going? We didn't have enough time to let it arrive. "It's been lovely to talk to you," I said. "But we have to get going now."

"Oh, okay," he said. "There are some leaflets and a donation—"

"Thanks," I interrupted, holding out my hand to shake.

He didn't move; not an inch. Left me hanging.

Had I offended him? I moved my outstretched hand closer to his body. My intention was clear, but he didn't react. I scrutinised his face. Had I misread some cue? Had he not enjoyed our short conversation? Should I have shown more interest in Hinduism? Evelyn seemed equally confused.

I put my hand down.

Wait. *His eyes.* They had never looked *at* us but *through* us. I waved my hand in front of his face. Again, no reaction.

He was blind. That had never happened before. Further proof of how many possible new endings there are to conversations with even the most familiar beginnings.

Outside, I looked around for Winnie. Someone had moved her. Or stolen her. Or made her invisible.

"You lost?" Evelyn asked, tapping her foot.

"No," I said, spinning in a circle. "Just spinning a bit. In a circle. Yeah, sometimes I like to spin in a circle and scratch my beard and look kind of confused."

"Why?"

"Why not?"

"With that logic you could justify anything."

"With your face you could justify anything! Oh wait, that one actually makes sense."

We laughed. "So..." she said, clearing her throat. "Just out of interest, can you ask your infallible mental map where the tuk-tuk's parked?"

"It's right over..." I spun once more, for luck. "It's *around*."

"Around where, though?"

"Well around here, of course. What a stupid question."

"Lead me to it."

"I could do that, no problem. But then you won't learn, will you?"

She planted her feet. "I've got time."

"No, we don't."

"True." Reluctantly, she pointed to exactly where, in the busy square, whoever had stolen the tuk-tuk had, at that very moment, returned it. It had a new neighbour: the majestic, heavily made-up, indisputably sacred cow.

I patted it affectionately as we passed.

"Hey, Winnie. You good?" I said, getting back behind her controls.

I pulled the starter lever. Nothing happened. I checked if we were in neutral. We were. "Winnie, don't leave me hanging, too." Had we left the engine on? Was the battery dead? No, I was always paranoid about that. And we'd not been in the temple very long. I let out the choke. "Breathe, Winnie."

Winnie didn't answer; she was the strong, silent type.

I tried the ignition sequence again, and this time the engine barked, whimpered, then cut out. I waited a few seconds and gave it another try. It cried out, screaming and screaming. But still it refused to turn over.

"WINNIE! NO! BE A GOOD GIRL!"

Fortunately, those screams were loud enough to interest a few of the dozens of men loitering nearby, and several ambled over to assist. They're good eggs here.

Three men approached: two roughly our age, the third perhaps in his sixties and wrapped in a plum-coloured lungi. He took the driver's seat while the other two opened the back hatch.

*Three breakdowns in four days? Are we being too rough on poor Winnie?*

Not that yesterday had been a breakdown, really. Well, not of Winnie, anyway.

A few minutes passed. Evelyn and I stood uselessly nearby, squabbling over who had, yet again, drunk so much of the collective water. A shout went out from the two men at the back: the man in the front turned the key.

The engine groaned, then cut out.

A shout from the back. The man in the front turned the key.

The engine groaned, then cut out.

No shout from the back. The man in the front turned the key anyway, and a spark shot from the engine, electrocuting one of the men working to repair it. He flew backwards in the air and crashed into the side of the heavily made-up cow, who knocked against the pole of a stall of household goods, which rained tins, pots, and saucepans down onto the ground.

I dropped our water bottle (yet more water waste) and ran towards the man. I'd learnt from my mistake on training day —I should help, even if I didn't know how. The cow mooed angrily as the electrocuted man lay in a heap, his eyes rolled up into his skull. His helper slapped him in the face, trying to rouse him. A crowd formed around us. Although I'd rushed to his rescue, I had no idea how to do so, and so stood once more, doing nothing with a strong air of purpose.

We had the square's attention now, and people spilt from the temple to watch. We'd had far too much attention lately. Everyone wanted to know what had happened. Why were saucepans scattered over the ground? Why was a man unconscious? Why was a cow in makeup?

Perhaps that last one was just me.

The older gentleman, who'd been in the driver's seat, tried to explain himself by gesticulating wildly. He accompanied the gestures with choice words in a language we didn't speak. Two more men were now at the engine, tinkering. Then they closed its cover.

*Is it fixed?*

People seemed more concerned about the cow than the unconscious man being slapped in the face. A face now also having water poured on it. The cow swayed its head from side to side. Its owner, Mr Cow, approached me, his eyes red and angry. "My cow," he said, pointing backwards. "You hurt my cow."

A group was forming behind him. The electrocuted person awoke, dazed, rubbing his head, as people pointed and berated him. Was it because he'd hit the cow? That wasn't really his fault. It wasn't really my fault, either. We were fate's patsies, he and I.

I looked at the cow: it seemed fine. If anything was stressing it out, it was having all these people around it being unnecessarily berating.

Or it was the makeup.

Another man approached. "Why you parked here?" he said. "This not place of parking. This is holy place." He signalled to the cow. "Holy cow."

I had a strong sense that we couldn't reason our way out of this one, as the people we were reasoning with were on the other side of a high, barbed wall of culture we had no hope of climbing. The electrocuted man was talking, and he pointed at us. The man who'd been in the driving seat—the one who'd caused all this with his errant key turn—had melted into the crowd.

It's dangerous to be in an accident here, where they still practice mob justice. The people near the accident look at the scene and apportion blame. They usually give this to whoever is the least injured. The punishment is beating them until they're at least as injured, usually more so. We'd been told that if we got into an accident, the best thing to do was get the hell out of there in a taxi and ask to go to the nearest police station.

If this crowd could be angry at a man whose only crime was getting electrocuted helping strangers, it could be angry at us.

"I'm sorry, sir," I said, raising my palms to Mr Cow and his friend. "I thought it was okay to park here."

Mr Cow was a small but powerfully built man. I'm a large, badly built man, no longer full of the vitality of youth but the dumpy mediocrity of fast-approaching middle age. I smiled while fingering at my tuk-tuk race lanyard. I was wearing my official brown tuk-tuk Rickshaw Rally shirt. I straightened it. "Just a misunderstanding," I said, as a few more people arrived from the temple. Mr Cow took a step towards me and I moved to the side, towards the crowd, hoping someone in it would help.

I stared him down, puffing out my chest, making the most of my height, feigning confidence and calm and innocence. I wasn't going anywhere. We would get this sorted. Where was Evelyn? If there was ever a time that we needed all the charm she didn't know she possessed, this was it.

Behind me, I heard a dull thud.

Mr Cow and his friend stepped closer; they were just half a metre away now. I looked around for somewhere I could run to, should I need to. I silently prayed to Hanuman, the part-man-part-monkey god. I liked him the best: I was more monkey than man. I should have taken that leaflet. I should have stuffed some of those shiny new banknotes into the temple's donation box. I should have found a pot as big as Wales to hide in.

Behind me, another thud. Then a yell. A woman's yell. Then a louder thud that morphed into a low, rumbling groan.

Mr Cow raised his hands to my chest.

*BEEP BEEP BEEP*

I turned to see that, somehow, Evelyn had found the strength to start Winnie, had swung her round, parting the crowd like Moses the sea, and was racing towards us into the back of Mr Cow and Angry Man.

*BEEP BEEP BEEEEEEEEP*

They jumped to the side as she surged forward. "Get in!" she shouted, as she drew level, not slowing down, leaving me to turn and run as they gave chase.

How had she managed the starter lever? She was like those women who lift cars off their babies.

"Quick!"

I sprinted for Winnie, grabbed her frame, and hoisted myself up to fall ungracefully into a part-man-part-monkey heap on the backseat. Evelyn took the corner fast in second gear, and Winnie's left wheel lifted off the ground before bouncing down as we sped out of the square and away from danger.

She had saved us. She had saved us again.

30

# MURUDESHWAR

"How you doing up there?" she shouted. We'd increased the shifts from one and a half hours to two.

"Yeah, fine."

"Well, your shift's over, so just pull in whenever."

"Oh, okay. I mean I could also carry on, if you like? We're almost there."

"No, it's my turn."

"Yeah, it's just, we're making good progress and everything."

"*Pull in.*"

It had taken four days, but we'd gone from hating driving Winnie to actively trying to sneak extra time in her front seat. Afraid we were still being chased by the angry residents of Udupi, we'd been driving like the wind, which is an expression that makes more sense in a place where there is wind. We'd been driving fast, basically.

"Wo-ah," I said, as I turned us off the motorway and caught sight of an enormous Shiva statue sitting high on the rocks, guarding the scruffy coastal town of Murudeshwar. Its back was to the rippling Arabian Sea. To say that the thirty-seven-metre-high, four-armed man in the lotus position was out of place would be to concede there was a place such a thing could belong.

And Murudeshwar was barely a place. It seemed to have more stray dogs than permanent residents. It was, mostly, this statue, the curved beach behind it, and the businesses between them, which thrived as a result of both.

We arrived at the hotel at 2pm, in seventh place, before Aarav had even arrived. "Photo," said a man with his two neatly dressed daughters, as we unpacked our stuff from Winnie.

"Sure," Evelyn said, as the girls moved between her and me, prising us apart with the sharp points of their youthful elbows. The youngest daughter continued prodding my sides, pushing me further left in her attempts to nuzzle closer to Evelyn. How much space did they need? By the time she'd finished exiling me, there was a metre of space between us. I wouldn't be in the photo. The father smiled and took it anyway.

*Oh, wait...*

It can be loud when the penny drops. This time it was deafening. A montage of the hundreds of times people had asked us for photos shuffled quickly through my mind, like cards in a croupier's hands. I remembered how something had always felt off during these brief encounters. I'd thought it was because taking a photo is always awkward: hitting pause on a moment to create something you hope will later allow you to hit play in your memory. But that hadn't been it. It had been awkward because none of the people asking had wanted me there. They'd just wanted *her*. They'd tolerated me.

Why had it taken me a week to notice?

*Ego.* Here it was again, defending me, keeping reality out. Telling me I mattered. A new family arrived and wanted a photo. I took the last of our bags from Winnie. My absence only seemed to increase demand. People finished paying their respects to Shiva, saw us in our novelty vehicle, and wanted to know about the race.

"It's okay to say no," I said, once I'd finished with Winnie.

"I don't mind," she said.

"You do though."

"It makes them happy."

There is no equally distributed resource on earth: not money, intelligence, height, beauty, attention, hair colour, or common sense. Evelyn had been given prodigious natural gifts. As had I, but she made more effort to share hers. In the future, I decided I would too.

"I'll check us in," I said. It wasn't until I was at the reception desk that I realised I'd not asked if I could stay in her room again. We were still getting on fantastically well. But wouldn't it be presumptive? More than suggestive? With perhaps a hint of ambush? I stepped away from the desk towards the door. She was giggling, having her legs hugged by a young boy while his proud mother took a photo. I could have gone and asked. But that would have put her on the spot, would have forced her to say yes.

I walked back to the desk and booked a second room.

31

## THE BEACH

Murudeshwar Beach was crowded with bathers frolicking in the calm of low tide. The women were clothed. The men had allowed themselves bare chests. Other than a few tuk-tuk racers, we were the only Western tourists on the beach, and the locals greeted our arrival with the usual warm enthusiasm.

"Hello."
"Namaste."
"Where from?"
"Germany. You?"
"Mumbai. Where go?"
"Goa. From Trivandrum."
"Good. Far."
"Yes."
"Swimming?"
"Yes!"
"Swimming."
"Yes."

We dropped our stuff on the sand and ran for the water, elated that the day's work was over and we still had all this time for play. This trip had badly lacked it. We lay in the shallow water as the piddly waves shunted us back towards the beach. When a larger one rolled in, a man in a white shirt threw his arms up in the air and whooped.

So, we whooped.

So, more people whooped.

Giant Shiva was facing the wrong way and missing all the fun.

Floating on my back, I thrust out my arms and legs and gazed appreciatively up at the cloudless sky, yellowing at its edges like old paper. I thought about Trivandrum, about how long ago that felt. The next waved rolled lazily in, spinning me forty-five degrees and knocking me into Evelyn, who sat with her knees to her chest, staring at the horizon through sunglasses.

"Hey!"

Most of the race was behind us now. The corners of my mouth marched upwards. I was delighting in being both with her and all these other people, in being splashed not only by tiny waves but also by the large enthusiasm for them.

It's easy to become jaded in this life. The best antidote to it is to surround yourself with people who understand their good fortune better than you do. Because not only are most places in-between places, but our lives are comprised mostly of in-between moments: checking our phones to see if we have any new messages; washing up dinner plates; scrubbing at coffee-stained teeth; tying the strings of slowly ripping bin bags; checking again to see if anyone in this world cares enough about us to send us a damn message.

The small things *are* the big things, served in bite-sized chunks. While it's always tempting to chase peak experiences, life is 99 percent trough experiences. It's what we do with these that determines how we feel most of the time.

I realised I'd got something very wrong in my life. I had always thought the goal was to seek out things that *made* you enthusiastic. That enthusiasm was a response to pleasing stimulus. This is wrong. Enthusiasm is a gift that you give: a conscious choice you make to lift something up from that trough. The thing itself isn't important. What you make out of it is. Therefore, Peak Theory also had to be wrong—the thing doesn't decide how much I enjoy it. I decide, every time I experience it.

Enthusiasm is its own reward.

## 32

# MATE

A light perfume of cinnamon laced the air as Evelyn and I joined the others at a pretty beachfront restaurant for dinner. It was a special night: for the first time, we all knew we'd finish the race. That while its end wasn't yet in sight, it was firmly on the map: just a hundred-and-change kilometres away.

Tonight, we would eat, drink, and celebrate our proximity to it.

Places with warm climates don't understand how fortunate they are. Al fresco dining sprinkles meals with a spice of refinement so pungent it should be listed as an ingredient.

We ordered cocktails and many dishes of spinach and lentils and spicy baked cheeses and just about an entire bakery's worth of breads with exotic names we mispronounced. While we waited for the feast to arrive, I excused myself and headed for the bathroom, where I found Lance swaying as he peed into the long metal trough. He was, literally, having a trough experience. He and his racemates had probably been drinking since two.

"Alan!"

"*Adam.*"

"Yeah, mate. How's it hanging?"

"Fine."

"Right on, aye." He started whistling "Waltzing Matilda."

I stopped at the far end of the urinal, as etiquette dictated. I unzipped. It wasn't easy to get started, but after a few seconds I relaxed enough and relieved myself, staring ahead at the white ceramic tiles.

"*Woah*," Lance said. "Dude!" He'd angled himself to face me and was looking down at my penis. "My dick rules over your dick."

Time stopped. I turned, and my eyebrows crashed together. "What the fuck?!"

Sometimes you're caught in a moment you can neither believe is happening nor do anything to stop. "Dude," he said again, emphatically. "It rules!"

I'd heard the best thing to do to a flasher is to laugh at them. To throw back your head, cackle, point, and say *is that all you've got?*

I was being flashed, but I was also flashing. And the flasher was heckling *me*—there was no playbook for this. I had no idea how to react. I juggled the options quickly in my mind and decided it was best not to show my annoyance. "Good for... you," I said, and turned back to the tiles.

He laughed again, returned to his whistling, then left without washing his hands. As I stood at the sink, washing mine, I looked at myself in the mirror. I'd hoped I wouldn't recognise what I saw there, but I did. I recognised it too well. It was a coward. I had backed down once more. Throughout my life I'd failed tests of masculinity like this one. It explained why, now, at thirty-four, I still felt like a child playing dress-up.

I balled up the paper towel and lobbed it at the bin. It missed.

In French there's an expression—*L'esprit de l'escalier* ("the wisdom of the staircase")—for the thing you should have said at the time but only think of later. As I walked outside, that wisdom arrived: *It's a shame that with your personality you'll have such little chance to use it.*

Too little, too late. I trudged back towards our table, my body twice as heavy under the weight of self-hatred. Lance was in my seat, grinning up at me, slapping his tongue against his bottom lip.

I balled my fists. "You're in my seat."

"Am I? *Oh*. No problem, just pull up another, aye."

"*You're* the problem."

"*Mate*," he said sarcastically, turning to Evelyn, giving her a *can-you-believe-this-guy-getting-all-pissy-over-nothing* look.

Adrenaline pulsed through me, and I grew a few centimetres. "You can pull up a chair. But this one is mine." At some point, doing the wrong thing is better than doing nothing at all. I was through with doing nothing at all.

"Oh, come on," Evelyn said, with the flat tone of a tired mum splitting up quarrelling children. She moved her chair to the right and pulled up a new one beside it. Lance hopped gleefully across from my seat into the new one, since it was nearer to her.

I sat.

I stared ahead.

I fumed.

My Ego had been defeated, my fortress breached, and something precious stolen: my self-respect.

## 33

# RACE DAY FIVE: MURUDESHWAR TO CANDOLIM

"Morning, Winnie," I said, giving the old girl an affectionate pat on the roof. "You sleep well? It's good to see you."

Evelyn frowned. "You're in a good mood."

"Uh-huh," I said. This wasn't true, but I intended to make it so—to give the day my enthusiasm and see what it returned, while trying to forget the previous evening and all my various deficiencies. "I'm in a good mood because I get to spend another day with Winnie. And it's not far today, right? So, there's no need to rush. And then we're in Goa, which means beaches, partying, and not having to hunt around for alcohol. And the race is over."

Kerala had been flirting with prohibition. Some towns were dry while others had just a few licensed bottle shops, or the odd tourist hotel with an exemption. Each evening, the group dinner would be held wherever we could be sure of getting alcohol.

"Hmm," she said. "I'm not sure what to do with Happy Morning Adam. It's like getting one of those offers that's a bit too good to be true. You don't trust it."

"You don't trust me?"

She scratched her arm. "Weirdly, I do. Actually. You know. *Huh.*"

"Do you want to start?" I asked, unsure exactly what any of that sentence meant.

"Yep."

I climbed into the back and reached for the Bluetooth speaker. "So it shall be."

Day five brought something new: changes in elevation. Most of the trip had been flat, yet suddenly the ground leapt upward, making Winnie's engine wheeze and cough. The views grew ever more spectacular as we crested steep hills then whizzed through descents that would have seen us soiling ourselves on day one. Now, these descents were as warmly welcomed as the visit of a long-forgotten childhood friend. I lay across the backseat, poking my feet out the side, my bag behind my head as a pillow, enjoying the views, nodding along to the music, gazing occasionally at Evelyn. Tufts of her hair escaped their clips and blew like streamers in the breeze.

Tuk-tuks are a triumph, like riding on a really rubbish, heavily polluting magic carpet. We had to give Winnie back at the end of the day. That was another thing I was trying not to think about.

---

"Can you put your damn phone away?" I said.

"Can you put your damn face away?"

*Huh, so my humour is rubbing off on her.*

We had so much time, we'd taken a detour to Agonda—a quiet beach about twenty minutes from Palolem, Goa's famous hippy beach town. Under a thatched roof we sat side by side looking out at a vista shared by humans, dogs, and cows. In the distance, a half-dozen islands shimmered in the water. An elderly woman in a peach-coloured bikini and red sarong did tai chi, miming in an ancient language we didn't understand. Locals played beach cricket between red flags warning potential swimmers that "this surf bites." I squelched my bare feet deeper into the warm sand, excited for all the food I'd ordered to arrive.

The day's driving was going wonderfully—quiet roads, beautiful nature, and a paltry distance to cover. If only every day could have been like this. Lunch arrived: a delicious, rich Goan fish masala and a tandoori lobster served on two giant banana leaves.

"Do you cook Indian food?" Evelyn asked.

"I don't cook."

"Ever?"

"I don't even own a cookbook. I just slice fruit and roast vegetables."

"Weird."

"The food here..." I said. "How do they make it so good?"

"Butter."

"That's it?"

"That's it."

"Good on 'em, I say. *Butter*."

"Butter is a misunderstood vitamin."

I stopped eating. "Hang on a minute..."

"What?"

"Don't *what* me all innocently. That 'misunderstood vitamin' line."

"Good, right? I just thought of it," she said, with a butter-wouldn't-melt look.

"I've heard it before." Even if butter didn't melt, it might still plagiarise.

She shook her head. "No."

I pulled out my phone, willing to break my own rules. "AHA! '*Alcohol is a misunderstood vitamin.*' *P G Wodehouse*. You stole the last part of it."

"No, I'm pretty sure I just…" Her nose twitched. "That's… that's… time*ist*!"

I punched the air. "Yes! Finally. You see I'm right. Timeism is real! And also one of the greatest injustices of our time. *Literally.*"

"I wouldn't go that far."

"How far would you go?"

"I'm willing to admit you have a point. It's just blunt."

We returned to our delicious, buttery food. "Are you going to do anything different when we get back?" I asked.

"*Erm.*" Her eyes narrowed. "Why?"

"I thought the trip might have given you some clarity on things?"

*Like how you've let work take over your life? Or how much you want to rip all my clothes off, right here and now, in front of all these people?*

"I don't know. I'm not sure I trust big epiphanies and revelations."

"Why not?"

"It just feels like if everything can swing in one direction, it's just as likely to swing back again. That it's more about changing something than what you change. Maybe. I mean. I don't know. Are you going to change something?"

I thought about in-between things, people, and places, and about the gift of enthusiasm. The path was clear. I just had to stay on it.

"Nope. I'm going to do all the same things—*better.*"

34

---

## FATE JINXERS

It had seemed impossible that this moment would ever arrive. Yet, here we were, looking out from it into a future beyond it, about to flip its tense from present to past.

One thousand kilometres.
Five days.
Two strangers.
One tuk-tuk named Winnie.

We'd made a great team. That team was about to break up. I'd thought I'd feel elated to no longer be responsible for Winnie and to be free of mandated 6am starts and twelve-hour race days. Instead, I was melancholic, pinched by uncertainty. Winnie was no longer an opponent to fight: she was family. And no Winnie meant no Evelyn…

"So," Evelyn shouted back at me. "I don't want to be a fate jinxer, but it's looking like we'll finish this stupid race," she said, while changing gear, honking, and overtaking a car on the wrong side of the road. I've read we're most attracted to our partners when we see them flourish at something. To see Evelyn drive Winnie was to watch someone made new. Not that my attraction to her needed any encouragement at all.

"Yeah, it's amazing how quickly you get good at something when you do only that for a week," I said.

It wasn't only my feelings for Winnie that had intensified. The ones I had for Evelyn were enormous, confusing, freewheeling, maddening. This experience had bonded us. We knew we worked well together in enclosed spaces, on little sleep, and under great stress. We'd seen each other sweaty, tired, angry, hungry, bleeding, clutching stomachs, and running for toilets. Soon we'd go back to Berlin, where we had none of the same friends, opposite schedules, and different hobbies. Was it the end of our story? Would we see each other again?

She drove on, humming to herself, her gear changes smooth, the engine quiet and pliant. In five minutes, it would be my turn to drive again. My last shift.

A dirty-grey bus hurtled alongside, causing Winnie to tremble and cower like a defecating dog. I scowled at its cocky young driver, who was accelerating onto the wrong side of the road, hammering his horn, certain of his right to dominate. Seeing Evelyn, a passenger in the bus did a double take and scrambled for his phone. I coughed on another cloud of dust.

A cow ambled out from a scrubby, overgrown field into the path of the overtaking bus. A jolt of adrenaline surged up my neck, snapping me straight. The bus had seen the cow but couldn't brake in time and return to the left-hand lane because we were blocking it.

"BRAKE! BRAKE!" I shouted.

It was too late...

"Kill a cow and they'll kill you." Aarav had warned us.

"BRAKE! BRAKE! BRAKE!" I screamed, as every horn around us sounded an alarm. With no other choice, the bus swerved its front half back into our lane, which sent its rear-half swinging out and then back towards us.

Evelyn screamed. I closed my eyes, waiting for the sick

crunch of metal and bone.

*How under control is my life now?*

Death is the ultimate destroyer of routine. The permanent all-inclusive holiday. The final great trip into the unknown. This was how it would end? With her, but without her knowing what I felt for her?

What an incredible waste.

Time decelerated to a slow crawl. *This is the part where my life should flash before my eyes, isn't it?* It didn't. The past stayed just that. No worst-of or best-of reels looped. What I did see—as my subconscious lit up with fear—were flashes of a future I wanted with her: of the places we'd live, the trips we'd take, the family we'd build, the stories we'd tell.

I was here for her. I had always been here for her. I was just scared of being found out again. Of failing. Of being rejected. Of giving up the keys to the fortress. Of drowning in Doubt.

While all of that was scary, the thought of losing her was even more terrifying. You can't protect yourself from the world. It's folly to even try. I wanted more tests like this race. I wanted to lust and love and make old mistakes new ways. I wanted to care for someone and have them care for me. I wanted to have children someday, and for them to have hair like hers. I wanted her semi-relevant stories, inappropriate winks, feminist rants, weird jokes, smiles, and ridiculously attractive hair tousles. I wanted to be lit by her quiet, unassuming light and watch her hypnotise everyone around her. I wanted to help her see herself as I saw her. And discover how she saw me.

I hadn't told her this.

Not really.

Properly and confidently.

Not with certainty and conviction. I'd always backed down. Just as I'd backed down from Lance.

If we survived this, it was time.

35

# BYE TO WINNIE

The tuk-tuk thudded to a stop, throwing me forwards out of my seat and over the metal divide, where I head-butted Evelyn in the shoulder. She yelled as I fell backwards and tumbled down into the back footwell.

Her screaming stopped.

I unclamped my eyes.

*Are we dead? Is this Heaven or Hell?* It was both: it was India.

"OW," she said. "Fuck. You okay?"

"No." I grabbed the seat back and pulled myself up. "You?"

"WE ALMOST DIED," she said, sucking air into her lungs. Up ahead, the bus shrank from view.

"What happened?"

"I braked. We missed it by..." She held up two fingers with a tiny gap between them.

"What happened to the cow?" I asked.

"Darted back at the last minute." She shook her head. "That bus."

"You did good," I said. We got out and hugged by the side

of the road.

She wiped a tear from her eye. "I don't think I can—"

"Shall I take over?" *She would say no.*

"Yeah, if that's okay?"

"That's okay."

"You did good," I said again. She looked at the ground and said nothing, continuing to massage her shoulder blade.

How close had we come to dropping down the rabbit hole? To this becoming one of those monumental moments? Where something happens that you can't take back?

Back on the road, I drove slowly. Our confidence, my hip, and her shoulder were bruised. Suddenly we were nervous again. It's not that you completely overcome fears, I realised. That framing is wrong; too absolute, too binary. Fears are more like Manish's metaphorical snake. If you work hard, you can get them under control, tame them, hold them firmly by the neck. But they're not beaten. Relax too much, get a little too cocky, and they'll wriggle free and bite you. If I was always a little apprehensive about driving, it would be because apprehension is a form of respect. It shows you're aware of the damage you could do to others and yourself. It's okay to feel fear. The important thing is not to let that fear paralyse you. It didn't anymore.

"What's the name of the hotel?" I asked.

"The Oceanic. Next right."

A dozen flags flew from its entrance, but only one was black and white and waved by Aarav.

It was over.

I parked and sat back, savouring the moment. A final turn of the key in the ignition. We had survived. Winnie had survived. The people of India had survived.

"I'll miss her."

"Me too."

The three of us sat together in a long, meaningful silence

broken only by my loud inhales. For a moment, I wanted only to enjoy her scent: a mix of hot leather, sweat, petrol, and potential. I rubbed my hand across her seats, turned her dials, flicked her switches while Evelyn took a final few photos.

"She's been good to us," Evelyn said.

"She sure has."

"Everyone else tried to kill us, that's obvious, but I have a feeling Winnie was mostly on our side, all in all."

"I'm going to miss you, girl," I said, running my hand slowly along her dashboard. Winnie said nothing, struck dumb by the intensity of her feelings for us. Either that or she was an inanimate object. Evelyn wrapped her arms over her roof, giving her a final enthusiastic embrace. I joined from the other side, wrapping my arms over the roof and taking Evelyn's hand.

Our first joint project was over. It reminded me of how the hard part of anything isn't the doing—it's the saying yes. *Yes* creates momentum, a commitment, and a fear of failure that propels you forward. That had propelled us forward. That had stopped us from quitting no matter how much we'd wanted to. And we'd wanted to almost every minute until the end of day three.

Sonia drove into the car park, came to a slow, measured stop, then put the tuk-tuk into reverse (so we had reverse?) and casually, without looking over her shoulder, swung a perfect arc back into the space.

"Wow," Evelyn said. We'd been so busy focusing on our own fears we'd not noticed all the people around us overcoming their fears, completing their challenges.

"Pretty good, right?" she said, climbing out.

"Love," said Manish. "That was hotter than a holiday on mars."

We walked inside. There was an awards ceremony to attend, and a woman to woo.

36

## THE ROAD TO RUIN

"You look..." I whistled as Evelyn turned in a circle, swishing up the edges of a red satin dress. There was absolutely no reason for her to be this beautiful. It was a thick layer of icing on an already compelling cake of personality.

The awards ceremony was being held at a hotel ten minutes away, directly on the beach. We set off wandering a maze of alleys. Businesses bunch in India, and this was the mechanic-and-scrap-metal area. Five minutes later, we emerged from it onto a busy road, where we waited with a group of pedestrians for a gap in traffic. Evelyn was behind me.

"Hey," she said, as we walked out into the road. It was the end of the workday; the streets were busy.

I turned around. "What?"

"Nothing. Ugh." She strode past me, almost running to the other side of the road. I chased after her and, on the pavement, pulled her back by the arm. "What happened?"

"Some guy grabbed my ass."

I shot round, staring into the faces of the nearest men. "WHO WAS IT?"

She sighed. "It doesn't matter."

"It matters. Of course it matters. They can't get away with that." I swallowed. "Why didn't you shout?" I could hear my pulse in my ears; every sense was amplified. "They have to know that women will scream, shout, kick, punch."

"Yeah, and then what do you think happens?"

"People will help you."

She crossed her arms. "That's cute. What happens is you get more attention you don't want. Even if they find him, he'll deny it. Then people will comment on how you're dressed. On whether you've been drinking. On whether you encouraged him. What follows is usually worse than the thing itself."

"This happens a lot?"

"*Yes.*"

"But if you don't report it, how can it get better?"

"It won't get better if I do."

"He can't get away with it."

"He did." She let her hands fall to her sides.

"I think I'm starting to understand why you're so distrustful of men."

"*What?*" She lifted a fist then dropped it. "I'm not. It's a small percentage of men who harass and lie and cheat. I've met some spectacularly great men. And some spectacularly awful, petty women." She wiped a tear away with the back of her hand. "You're great. I think that took me some." She swallowed then wiped at another tear. "It's not. I don't know. I assumed it was just an act you were putting on."

"Evelyn." I took her hand.

"Don't," she said, pulling it away. "You don't want me. You want your ending."

"Oh, come on." I stamped my foot. "That's ridiculous. I'm not your ex-boyfriends. You should see someone about your trust issues."

"About those..." She broke eye contact. "I think maybe you're right. But I haven't told you all the reasons."

"You don't owe me any explanations."

"You're not the only one who just went through a breakup." Her teeth scraped her lip. "He was a compulsive liar. As in, every single thing he said was untrue. Other than his name. I think that was true. Turns out he had another girlfriend the whole time. Pregnant. I don't think you know what that's like. To give someone something and then have them slowly twist it and break it in front of you while swearing that everything is fine, that they want that thing, that no, they're not twisting anything at all. That it's all in your head. That you're paranoid. That you have *trust issues*."

So she wasn't an open book. She was open with what didn't matter but protected the rest, just like everyone else.

"I think he sort of broke normal for me."

I paced back and forth rubbing the back of my neck. I wanted to find this guy and go Middle Ages on him. Even if I couldn't protect myself, I wanted to protect her. No amount of Doubt would stop me from doing that. And not because it was my "job as a man" but because she deserved to be treated by the world as she treated it: with kindness, warmth, and compassion. The intensity of the emotions surging through me was as surprising as it was irrational. Evelyn and her ex were no longer together. He was history. We were the present. And the odds of this particular present happening? Infinitesimally small. Everything had to have played out exactly as it had for us to get here. If he were a good person, a truth teller: no me, no us, no this.

"I'm sorry," I said. "That would have left some scars."

"It makes you question, well... I won't make that mistake again."

I thought back to that first phone call. How she'd tried to make it seem as if she were doing *me* a favour by letting me come. I thought about how difficult it was for her to depend on me, even for simple things like carrying her bag, haggling on her behalf, or pulling the starter lever for her. Suddenly her behaviour made sense—if you never rely on anyone, you can't be disappointed when they let you down. Independence looks like strength, but it's often just fear masquerading as indifference. I recognised the behaviour because I did it too. I never asked for help if there was any way to avoid it. I found it hard to let people in. I bolted as soon as I felt cornered. I always needed to be in control. I'd just never understood exactly why until now.

"You could have told me sooner, you know? I wouldn't have judged you. I might have even been a bit softer on your need for capital *T* Truth."

"I know I could have, but why? I'm not a victim. I don't need anyone's pity. I'm doing just fine, most of the time."

"I know."

"Even if I don't always look it."

"*I know.*"

"And I don't want to be some flawed but lovable character in a book. A plot device. A story arc. A protagonist's prize. Another thing you'll want until you have it and the Happy Ever After has faded out to the credits."

"You're a part of this story, though. *We* are a part. A more interesting part than the race, I think."

"Exactly! The will-they-won't-they! The reader needs a satisfactory conclusion."

"I'm not writing a book," I said, without knowing if it was true. I was always writing a book, whether in notepads on my knee or in the scrap pages of my mind. It was a compulsion, the only way I knew how to make sense of the world. Evelyn wasn't the only workaholic.

"The guy needs to get the girl. Adam needs his Eve. You don't want me, you want that. And I don't want to be that. I was doing fine before you came along, and I'll be just fine once this is all over." She lifted her chin and walked away.

## 37

## THE CLOSING PARTY

The room's white walls, tablecloths, and fabric-covered seats worked hard to sell an innocence that doesn't exist in the world. This was a room for weddings. It was not the room I needed at this moment. I needed something for a wake.

"Well." Standing on the left-hand side of the stage at the front of the room, Aarav grinned. The cult leader without the cult. Jones without a town. "I know I've spent most of the week making fun of you, because..." He flicked out his tongue. "*Fun*. But I also know you were shit scared. This was a really mind-wrecking, crazy thing to do. We're actually just really proud of you."

I spotted Evelyn on the other side of the aisle that ran through the centre of the room, sitting with the women from Bahrain. Pamir stood to the right-hand side of the stage looking his usual blend of forlorn and forsaken. It was over for us but not for him. For him, it would never be over. He was running his own race, and he'd always be in last place.

"Pamir, get over here?" said Aarav, waving him across.

He shook his head.

"*Pamir.*"

Pamir sucked in his lips and tugged on the edges of his moustache. Aarav waddled over and enveloped him in a wide hug. It was like watching a toddler rugby-tackle Santa. "Come here, big guy," he said, dragging him across the stage as everyone clapped and cheered. We all liked Pamir. It was a shame he didn't like himself, that he was a fellow mental masochist.

"Think back to how you were in that field," said Aarav. "And now? It's an incredible change in just a week, no? So give your bloody selves a big round of applause. You deserve it."

Why was he being so... nice?

"You fools," he added, to restore balance to the universe.

Pamir bent to whisper in his ear. "Ah, yes, thanks, Pamir. You probably want to know who won, right?"

I looked around. No one seemed that interested in who had won. It hadn't been a topic at dinner each evening. This challenge was personal, not collective. About finishing, nothing more.

"Let's start with the teams who barely completed any of the daily challenges and limped over the finish line with about ten minutes of daylight left. We're not sure exactly what order they finished in because we were too lazy to count, and what does it matter?"

Pamir took a piece of paper out of his pocket and unfolded it. "The Frankfurt Samurais, Karacol Alventus, Applewine Express, the 4 O'Clockers, and Win Diesel."

The group gave us a sympathetic clap. I looked over to Evelyn but she was looking ahead, until Lance reached over and clasped Evelyn's shoulder, and she turned and smiled. I shook off my annoyance, what did it matter now? Her cheeks were puffy, but she'd fixed her modest makeup. They called more team names and we clapped. Sonia and Manish finished fifteenth. Mr and Mrs Outsourcing came tenth. The Malaysian was twelfth. Lance and his crew came sixth. The winners were two amateur racers who'd finished so early each day we'd barely even seen them.

"Now." Aarav moved his hand in a slow circle. "There's also a special community award." He looked up lovingly at his gentle giant of a partner. "Do you want to?"

Pamir considered it and all the ways it could be booby-trapped. "Well." He made a short pit stop to frown. "I know you've not heard much from me at each pep talk. That's because I've had a lot to do. Unlike someone..." He turned to Aarav. "Who just had a lot to drink, mostly. But I got to spend a lot of time with you in the evenings and when you'd broken down. It was a great race, really. It's been a fantastic week. We've a special award we're calling the Community Award. It's for the boys who started the party each night. You know who I mean, I think. A really special group of lads who made everyone feel good. It would have been a much more boring race without them."

*Oh, please, God, no...*

His hand shot towards Lance. "Team Crouching Woman, Hidden Cucumber."

I sunk deeper into my seat; someone had turned the gravity up. Team Crouching Woman, Hidden Cucumber wore matching blue velvet suits. They leapt up and excitedly over each other like street dogs that had found a bucket of chicken. Eventually, after a solid minute of whooping and screeching, they made it to the stage to receive their trophy: a small golden tuk-tuk.

"Speech, speech, speech!" Pamir and Aarav chanted. The room slowly joined in as I sat silently willing the moment to be over, or, at least, for the stage to be trampled by a stray herd of angry elephants.

Lance clicked his jaw. "Yee, geez," he said, running his thick hand through his blond hair. "This has been fantastic, hasn't it, boys? Just one of the best things we've ever done, aye. And to get this award just tops it."

"Best week EVER!" shouted his teammate Tommo, as the third, Bazza, ran off the stage towards the bar.

"Come back, Baz!" Lance shouted.

Moments later, Baz raced down the aisle with a bottle of champagne over his head, popped the cork, and sprayed the stage and front row. I tried not to think about the cleanup costs. I tried not to think about how I was trying not to think about the cleanup costs.

They were rock, I was roll: roll over and give up.

"AAWOOOOOYYYY!" the three of them shouted, as they bounced up and down in a fraternal embrace, recording the special moment on Tommo's phone.

"And now we party!" shouted Lance.

The room cheered.

I crossed my arms.

I crossed my legs.

And I got very cross with myself.

It's easy to write off people like Lance and his friends, and I was often guilty of it. Of reducing them to simple caricature. Drunk, Lance was a noxious person. Sober, while he wasn't exactly a connoisseur of the human experience, sipping at life as if it were a fine wine, holding himself back so as not to get drunk on it, he had useful qualities. Qualities for which he and his teammates were being honoured. They immersed themselves in everything on offer at each moment. They were all-you-can-drink, all-or-nothing, smash-and-grab, happy-hour humans. People who get spontaneous tattoos, wake up in other people's underwear, and begin wild parties ended by men with badges and uniforms. There is a place for those people. I would simply prefer it to be far away from me.

Staff passed out drinks from copper trays. At the buffet I cut loose, gorging on samosas, pakoras, and mini skewers of chicken and lamb. I enjoyed every buttery mouthful. The food here was unparalleled.

"You are happy it's over, yes?" said Robert, as we stood to the side of the buffet. "Or perhaps not? To go back to normal life must be a relief, yes? Or maybe no?" I stuffed so much food in my mouth it looked as though I were preparing for hibernation. "Where is your girlfriend?"

"She's not my girlfriend."

"Mate," said Manish. "I'm going to miss you."

"Like a desert misses shade?"

We shared a sloppy hug. I broke it. I needed more alcohol.

I saw Evelyn at the bar. This didn't surprise me. I'd known she'd either be here or on the dance floor, doing effortlessly what for most of us would be hard work. The tension of our earlier argument sat heavily on my shoulders. I didn't want to carry it through the whole party. This was the end and ends should be highs, not lows. But I knew she wouldn't make the first move of conciliation; too awkward and confrontational. She'd blame herself, swallow it down and try to move on.

She was in conversation with Lance, who had his back to me. I hovered near them and signalled the bartender for a beer, positioning myself where I could make eye contact with her. Our eyes locked. Had it really been just two weeks earlier that we'd met in Berlin? Life had been simpler then. Almost 2D.

"Can I have a minute?" I asked.

Lance was a crane that swung slowly towards me. "Adam!" At least he'd dropped the Alan routine. "How you doing, *mate*?"

"Fine."

"You came joint last! Congrats!"

"Thanks, *mate*."

"I was just telling Evelyn that I'm thinking of going to Berlin soon."

"That's... nice?"

"Yeah. Isn't it, Evelyn?"

"Best wait until summer," she said. "It's a different city then. The best city. In winter it's average." She was free with information but guarded with her feelings. Had she recognised Lance and I were feuding?

"Anyway," he said to me. "Good chat." He turned back towards Evelyn and stepped to the right, blocking me off.

"Rude," Evelyn said, sidestepping to her left so she could see me again.

"Sorry?"

"You're shutting him out."

"Oh." Lance turned. "My bad. Didn't mean to do that."

"I think you did, though."

His neck bent forwards and his mouth slackened. *Is Evelyn sticking up for me? Is she making something awkward?* I took my chance. "Evelyn, can I have a minute?"

"You?" She smiled. "You can have two."

We took a seat on the back row of chairs, far from the stage, while staff in smart (white) uniforms began stacking them around us. I sat on my hands and watched as she tipped another gulp of red wine down her throat.

"I'm sorry," I said. "I don't know what it's like to be a woman, obviously. And I would never write about you if you didn't want that. And it's not my job to convince you of anything. Or to make you feel anything you don't feel just because I feel it. All this stuff is impeding what's important, which is that we did something hard and brave and stupid and yet we finished it anyway. Can we forget the rest for tonight, at least?"

She gave a short nod. "I can live with that."

Lance was hovering behind her, deliberately bobbing around in my field of view. "Lance is waiting for you."

She rolled her eyes. "I've met a lot of Lances."

"But the kiss?" We'd never mentioned the kiss.

"He kissed me."

"You kissed him back."

"No. I was just shocked mostly."

"You never mentioned it?"

"It wasn't in any way important." She raised her glass. "To Winnie."

"To Winnie."

38

# GOODBYE

The border guard thumbed the pages of my passport. He yawned, flashing coffee-stained teeth. This was his domain, and he'd yawn all he wanted. I was just the latest face in an endless gallery of potential rogues; the newest paperwork possessor requesting permission to enter a country I hadn't been born in.

The light on his miniature scanner flashed green. He handed back my passport. "*Willkommen.*"

"*Danke.*"

Evelyn and I passed into a kidney-shaped room, where we waited for our luggage to be spat unceremoniously from the mouth of one conveyor belt to another conveyor belt. Through the glass, a gloomy Berlin night threatened.

We'd lost both hours and seasons. *Ugh.*

Tiredness had numbed us into silence. We had talked little on the plane. The party had run late. Lance and I had avoided each other—I'd missed another chance to stand up for myself. There'd been much dancing and drinking and then a morning filled with goodbyes and a domestic flight that had led to two international ones. Now we were back where we belonged: in a city preparing to bury winter and dance on its corpse until the first sprouts of spring.

Our luggage thumped onto the belt, we heaved it onto a bus, and then lugged it down into the depths of the subway.

After India, Berlin felt impossibly solid, compact, and organised—like a game whose rules had been followed. A game long ago finished, its spoils shared.

Compared to Kerala, with its smiles, stares, and selfie requests, the subway felt as sterile as a doctor's waiting room. No one asked where we'd come from. Or where we were going. Or told us about a distant relative of theirs who was an optician in some in-between town an hour from Frankfurt. No one hewobbled or wheeled themselves through the carriage on a silver skateboard.

I passed the time wondering if Evelyn and I would see each other again. I could have asked, but she'd only have lied had the answer been no. And I had my story—the two strangers, the bar, the tuk-tuk named Winnie, Mr Cow, Aarav, Pamir, Lance, Manish, and Sonia. I could change her name, nationality, personality. I didn't need her anymore.

I still wanted her, though. But I couldn't make her want me.

"Boddinstrasse," said the recorded announcement. We stood and juggled our bags as the train slowed to a controlled stop. Nothing like Winnie's screeching, whining stops. The doors beeped then opened. We stepped out onto the freezing platform. Her exit was to the right, mine the left.

"So, yeah," I said. "See you around?"

She gave me a trademark Evelyn wink. "Sure."

My apartment was just five minutes away. In it, I'd be able to cross the last thing from the to-do list on my bedroom door. *Driving?*

I turned towards my exit. The train whooshed free of the station. I followed it.

## 39

## TWO WEEKS LATER

Life has very few cast-iron, universal truths. Almost everything is open to interpretation, is a matter of opinion not fact, and is about as changeable as a toddler's underwear. As I stood before my mailbox grappling in my pocket for its tiny key, I thought of one of these rare truths: nothing good comes via postal mail.

It hadn't always been so. There had been a glorious heyday of postcards, pen pals, love letters and chain mail promising riches. Now it was just administrative drudgery: bills and adverts from people who wanted to bring you things (sushi, mostly) or take things from you (removals companies, mostly). Sometimes I'd go a week without checking the mailbox, and when I did, I hoped it would be empty.

I slid the key into the lock and the white metal door creaked open. The inside was a jumble of items that included flyers, letters (two sushi, one removals), and an empty packet of cigarettes. I binned everything but three envelopes. The first had the logo of my health insurer. Seeing it, I felt acute pain in my wallet. The second was spam from the postal company itself, sending me a letter to get me to send more letters. I hoped the irony wasn't lost on them. I looked down at the third—a blue envelope, hand delivered.

Addressed to Stanley.

A lump formed in my throat. *Evelyn!* So, just occasionally, good things do still drop into postboxes. I'd heard nothing from her since we got back. I'd resolved that if there was to be further contact, she'd have to be its initiator. That way I'd know she wanted it. That she wasn't just being too nice to say no. The first few days I'd checked my phone a thousand times. I'd get up in the night, bleary eyed, jet-lagged, unable to sleep. Two weeks later, I was now slowly wrestling my attention and focus back under my control. If not my happiness. That would take much longer.

I tore at the envelope. Inside was a postcard. On the front she'd drawn a tuk-tuk. On the back was a date, a time, and a location.

*Sunday evening. 8pm. Prachtwerk.*

That was tomorrow. I knew Prachtwerk, a bar and event space a few streets from my apartment. I got out my phone and checked their website. Sunday's event was Stories with Spine: a storytelling event.

What story would she tell? The one about Winnie? The race? A new story? Another James story? Our story?

There it was again, that delicious, spiky feeling: possibility.

## 40

## SUNDAY EVENING

Prachtwerk was the opposite of Engels, the bar where we'd first met. Prachtwerk didn't hide the effort it was making. Prachtwerk was hot, and it knew it; knew you knew it; knew you knew that it didn't care you knew it. It knew a lot of things and was arrogant about every one of them. If it could have walked, it would have strutted. At its far end was a large raised wooden stage lit to oblivion by an enormous rectangular metal lighting rig.

I dug into my pocket and excavated my phone: 8:56. I was late, and it was already full. I hadn't been sure what to wear. I was sure I had nothing worth wearing, and on the way out I'd added the first new "to do" to my list since getting back from India: *Adult Clothes*. Just because I was a boy on the inside didn't mean I had to look like one on the outside.

I scanned the sea of heads. Hair like Evelyn's should have been easy enough to spot, yet I couldn't see it. But then, given the drama of the invite, surely she was performing, not merely part of the audience?

I took a seat near the back—if she was telling a story, I didn't want my goofy face putting her off.

The host appeared on the stage. He was a bearded American, but in this part of the city everyone was a bearded American. I wriggled on my small seat. Who had made it so small? So wriggly? I couldn't focus. I tutted a lot.

And then he said a name, and it sounded like... And then there she was, lit like an eighties-music-video star. She walked onto the stage carrying a goblet of white wine so large a guinea pig could have bathed in it. On first? She'd have asked for that slot. Would have wanted to get it over with. *What was it though?*

She put down her glass on the high table next to the microphone. Then she picked it up. Then put it down again then grabbed the microphone stand roughly. "Umm," she said. She picked up her glass again and took a gulp of wine, blinking out at the audience.

I sank lower as she smoothed the creases of a black dress with white polka dots. She cleared her throat. Storytelling was one of her strengths, but stages and public speaking? She left the limelight to her politicians. "So, err, this is a story about missed opportunity, I guess?" She laughed nervously.

I'd missed that laugh.

"So one night I entered this bar. It's actually pretty near here." She looked off to the left, the opposite direction of where my mental map had placed it. She'd be right, not me. "And anyway, I saw this guy. He looked a lot like a younger Stanley Tucci. I've always had a thing for Stanley Tucci. The only free seat was next to him, and I sat down. While I waited for my friend, I just knew he would talk to me. And unusually for me, I was okay with that. I don't know if any of you ever have this. When you look at someone and you just have this feeling about them. That they're your sort of person?"

There were a few murmurs and nods.

"He made a bad joke about being stood up."

*You made the bad joke, not me.*

"And so we talked. About boobs." She raised her hands to her chest. Slowed down the word *boobs*. The audience laughed.

"Right." She nodded. "It was weird, but the good kind of weird."

*The good kind of weird! Yes!*

"Because the friend I was waiting for had crashed her bike and was in the hospital. Which was a problem, because we were meeting to discuss final plans for a tuk-tuk race through India that we would start together a few days later."

"Suddenly I had no partner for that race. But I'd been working like crazy the previous weeks and I really, really needed this holiday. And a tuk-tuk race sounded so exciting. This guy—I'm going to call him Stanley since he didn't actually agree to be part of this story—he said maybe he could race with me? I ignored him, of course. It was a ridiculous idea. We didn't know each other. And there was no time to get to. But on the walk home that feeling was nibbling around in my gut that there was a story here, between him and me."

She took another sip. "He's a writer. Did I mention that? I should probably have mentioned that. So I downloaded one of his books. I've never told him I read any of them, but I did, and I liked it. He wrote about humans with a certain sympathy and compassion that spoke to me. Because that's also how I see them. And I really, really wanted to do this race. Anyway. I asked him to come. I told him later that I'd asked other people, but I hadn't."

*Huh. So the person who has a problem with lies lies.*

"He said yes. Which sounds ridiculous unless you've met him. Because he's kind of... *unusual*. And he has more free time than an eighteenth-century duke."

She paused for more laughter.

"And so we raced. Us against twenty-three other teams. One thousand kilometres in five days. All day, every day. Whenever I was struggling, he took over. Whenever he was, I did. We were a great team. Now, I have terrible taste in men. I've never been good at relationships. They're like a foreign country that never gives me a visa. I'm always on the outside, somehow, peering over the fence, trying to work out how everyone else gets in so easily and has such a lovely time strolling around holding hands and staring lovingly into each other's eyes. And yet, suddenly, randomly, I was *in* that country. For him, the scary part of that week was the race. For me, the scary part was *us*."

Another pause, as she chugged back a mouthful of wine.

"I didn't show him that, of course. And then the race ended. Oh, we came joint last and tuk-tuks are a lot of fun and so is India. Not the point, Evelyn." The story was unravelling slightly, or would have been for anyone who didn't know how her lightly scrambled brain worked. "All the time we were there, something was screaming and shouting and waving its arms around but I kept ignoring it. I've spent so much time hunting love, going on bad dates and persevering with bad relationships because I don't trust it when it hunts me. So I didn't trust it here. Didn't trust him when he said he wanted me. Didn't trust that I wouldn't just become some funny sidekick. I feared how he'd write about me and what it would do to how I see myself. And so I pushed him away. And I regret it. So now *I've* written our story. This is it, I guess. *Was it*." She paused. "I just wish I'd trusted in it enough to let it have a happier ending."

A second or two passed while people waited to see if the story was definitely over. If there wasn't, in fact, a happier ending to come? I rose from my seat and started clapping. Had she seen me? Or was it too dark back here? The audience joined in, and the applause became loud and enthusiastic. During it, I once again considered the possibility that this might really be one of those moments where someone gets what they want.

And that I might be that someone.

And that I would get her.

Which would mean men like me do get women like her. Which would mean she had to see something in me that I didn't see in myself. Which was the answer I'd been looking for to a question she'd asked during the race. *Yes, it is fair to ask someone to love you, even if you only sporadically love yourself.* Because we don't always know ourselves best. Over the trip I'd begrudgingly accepted that I didn't have a fantastic mental map. I now knew a little of how her mind worked. How hard it was on her. How much her ego skewed reality to her disfavour. How badly guarded her fortress was. I felt sure that, actually, I was a more rational appraiser of her qualities than she was. I found her to be very, very lovable. My job was to keep showing her how I saw her. And to let her do the same to me.

If everything really is that precarious, why fear a future we can't control? Why fear a story with a sad end that might have a beautiful start and middle?

She disappeared backstage. The next person told a story about a lost cat. The next about a Tinder date gone wrong. There was a break. Three more people. None as good as she'd been. And then the house lights came up. I expected her to appear at my side with a wink. Or to find her at the bar guzzling drinks. Neither happened.

I approached the host, who was conversing with the missing-cat lady. I could feel them preparing themselves for praise, putting on their most sincere modest smiles. *You liked little old me, really?*

"Did you see where Evelyn went?"

"Who?"

"Looks a bit like a young..." I stopped and pulled out my phone. It was finally time to see what Bette Midler looked like, young or old. I pulled up a picture. Google informed me she was an actress popular in the late sixties. *Huh...* The hair. The oval face. Those piercing eyes. I could see it. As a test, I showed him the photo.

"The tuk-tuk girl?" he said.

"Yep."

"Ah. I think she left."

Why would she do this and then just leave out the back door? She was a confusing human. But I was also a confusing human. We all are. She'd not want me to feel pressured, probably. She'd want me to have time to think things over, just as she'd taken the past two weeks. She'd not want to risk being rejected face-to-face. That would be the mother of all awkwardnesses.

I didn't need to think it over.

I knew what I wanted.

I had known since the beginning. Since I first saw her.

And I knew the right way to show her.

## 41

## BELGIUM

I pulled my phone out of my pocket and beamed three icons to space and back:
*A croissant*
*The Belgian flag*
*A question mark*

France didn't need us. France was doing just fine. *Belgium?* Belgium needed all the help it could get. And Evelyn and I were story people; if this was going to happen, it should happen in a similar vein to the weirdness with which our story had begun. To how it was developing. To how she was developing it. It was *our* story. Not mine. She had made the race happen and had invited me to join it. It was right that she'd told the story's first public draft.

A minute later I got a reply: a thumbs up.

*Where exactly is Belgium?* My mental map was letting me down once again. *Will we make it there by breakfast? Where does Evelyn live, exactly?*

There were more holes in the plan than Swiss cheese. And, possibly, Belgian cheese. Assuming such a thing existed. I asked for her house number and went to rent a car.

And then I was outside her building.

And then a shock of hair the colour of sunflowers at sunset in San Marino filled the passenger window.

And then the door opened.

And then there she was.

And that was nice.

"Hello," she said.

"Hello, stranger."

She got in and we grinned at each other for a while, possibly forty-five minutes.

"So," I said. "It turns out tuk-tuks are banned in Germany. This was all I could get. Swap after an hour and a half?"

"You bet."

"Nice story," I said, as I pulled away into traffic. *Driving? Fine. Nothing to me.*

Her phone rang. A ridiculous day and hour for a phone call in any other job. *New polls? Cat tax? Terror attack?*

She didn't move to answer it.

"Your phone?"

"I think maybe you were right about something. I've been using my job as an excuse for why my personal life is, well, kind of nonexistent. I'm making some changes. Healthier boundaries."

"That's big news."

"It's not the biggest. But we've a long drive ahead for that."

"What do Belgians eat for breakfast?" I asked.

"Who knows? Probably fries, knowing them."

Driving all the way to Belgium was a terrible idea, perhaps even a Dodo Idea, but our relationship was built on them. She leaned over and adjusted the radio.

"The 'Breakfast in France' story," I said.

"Yeah?"

"Something about it has been bugging me. Were *you* that girl?"

She let out a long, chunky laugh.

"I knew it! You lied!"

"*Lie* is a strong word."

So we were here again.

"How did you know?" she asked.

"You slipped a pronoun. Why would he kick you out? Are *you* an anti-vaxxer?"

*Could I date an anti-vaxxer? It would mean getting up more often to clean up the sick of our unborn children.*

"No. *He* was."

I howled with laughter. "No wonder he kicked you out. You would have gone all I-read-an-article on him."

It was good to be laughing together again. It impressed me how she was still taking chances, climbing—figuratively and metaphorically—into cars with near strangers.

"I didn't think I'd hear from you," I said.

"Yeah. I had some things to sort out."

"Like what?"

"My head." She angled herself towards me as we reached another killjoy red light. "It was a bit of a jumble in there. I think you're right. I had a few issues to work on, but there was no rush to do so until I met you."

"*Pff*. Everyone's got issues."

"Sure, you've got plenty."

"Everyone *except* me, I meant."

"Look," she said. "Enough. I want you. I want us."

My legs shook, which wasn't to the benefit of my driving, so I pulled into the entrance of a graveyard: a fitting place for a new start. "I need a minute."

"You can have two," she said, but then she gave me all of ten seconds. "This is the big emotional reveal. I hate that there is one. But there is. Now just listen and don't ruin it." She motioned back and forth between us. "We work, you and me. I couldn't believe it was real, I guess, and not another Man Mirage. I've done the start a lot. I'm not excited by the start and so I ignored the signs that there might be something beyond it. You're different. You're..." She paused. "You're like how you eat: worst to best."

*Did I make that bad a first impression?*

"I don't care how it plays out. I don't care how long it lasts, even. I thought I did but I don't. I don't even care if you want to write about us. I'm done caring what other people think about me. I know what you think about me, about us. And I trust you. I'm hoping, slowly, to trust myself. I ask for only one thing—honesty. Better five minutes of something real than months of make believe."

"I couldn't agree more."

She grabbed a fistful of my jumper and pulled me towards her. Our mouths met awkwardly. Someone had put too many teeth in them, it seemed. We recalibrated. That was better. Better than better; like being dipped in electricity. Time stopped, as it had when she'd entered that bar, when we'd danced at the race's opening party, and when we'd shouted stories at each other in those long hours in the tuk-tuk, laughing until the pits of our stomachs ached. One trip had come to an end, but another was about to begin.

*To Belgium, of all places.*

---

Thank you for reading! I never planned on becoming a memoirist. Yet, somehow, we're four books into the *Weird Travel* series.

Are you having fun? Would you like to read more stories like this one? The easiest way to show me is to leave a rating, review, or tell a friend about this book. As long as they're selling and people are enjoying them, I'll keep writing new ones.

In fact, the sequel to *Tuk-tuk for Two* is already out. It's called *After Happy Ever After*. I'm very proud of it and I hope to see you there. Here's it's blurb:

"I'm quitting my job," said the woman I was madly in lust with but had only just met.

"What?" I spluttered. "But you are that job?"

"I want to be someone else. Run away with me."

"But we just got back from India?" We had entered a tuk-tuk race as strangers, returning as unlikely lovers. "This is supposed to be our Happy Ever After. Can't we just enjoy it for a while?"

"Don't you want to see what's after Happy Ever After? Let's move to Istanbul. And I want to see Kurdistan."

Did she really want me to follow her to a region slipping into autocracy? To Turkey, a country our Government now explicitly recommended not to visit? And another it didn't acknowledge as existing?

"What's happening?" I said. "Who are you?"

She laughed. "Come with me and you'll find out. It'll be an adventure. And we can test this relationship."

I didn't know then that she had a secret. It was why she was in such a rush.

"Can I think about it?" I asked.

"Sure." She winked. "I'll give you fifteen minutes..."

After Happy Ever After is out now!

## ALSO BY ADAM FLETCHER

**- Non-fiction -**

Don't Go There (Weird Travel Series #1)

Don't Come Back (Weird Travel Series #2 and Writer's Digest Memoir of the year winner)

After Happy Ever After (Weird Travel Series #4)

Lost But Not Least (an exclusive free book for my newsletter subscribers)

Understanding the British

Fast Philosophy

**- Fiction (as Adam R. Fletcher) -**

The Death of James Jones, sort of

Printed in Great Britain
by Amazon